Winter 2000 Edition

COLLECTOR'S
VALUE GUIDE™

Ty® Beanie Babies®

Secondary Market Price Guide
& Collector Handbook

EIGHTH EDITION

Welcome To
The New Millennium

Ty® Beanie Babies®

Front cover (top to bottom): "1999 Holiday Teddy™" – *Beanie Babies*®, "The End™" – *Beanie Babies*®, "Ty 2K™" – *Beanie Babies*®

Back cover (top to bottom): "Peace™" – *Beanie Buddies*™, "Peace™" – *Beanie Babies*®, "Scaly™" – *Beanie Babies*®

Managing Editor:	Jeff Mahony	Creative Director:	Joe T. Nguyen
Associate Editors:	Melissa A. Bennett	Production Supervisor:	Scott Sierakowski
	Jan Cronan	Senior Graphic Designers:	Lance Doyle
	Gia C. Manalio		Susannah C. Judd
	Paula Stuckart		Carole Mattia-Slater
Contributing Editor:	Mike Micciulla	Graphic Designers:	Jennifer J. Denis
Editorial Assistants:	Jennifer Filipek		Sean-Ryan Dudley
	Nicole LeGard Lenderking		Peter Dunbar
	Joan C. Wheal		Kimberly Eastman
Research Assistants:	Timothy R. Affleck		Jason C. Jasch
	Priscilla Berthiaume		David S. Maloney
	Heather N. Carreiro		David Ten Eyck
	Beth Hackett	Web Graphic Designer:	Ryan Falis
	Victoria Puorro		
	Steven Shinkaruk		
Web Reporters:	Samantha Bouffard		
	Ren Messina		

ISBN 1-888914-62-9

CHECKERBEE™ and COLLECTOR'S VALUE GUIDE™ are trademarks of CheckerBee, Inc.

CheckerBee PUBLISHING
(formerly Collectors' Publishing)
306 Industrial Park Road • Middletown, CT 06457

www.collectorbee.com

TABLE OF CONTENTS

TABLE OF CONTENTS

WELCOME TO THE COLLECTOR'S VALUE GUIDE™

No one is sure what Ty Inc. has in store for the future of *Beanie Babies*®, so for now, let the Winter 2000 Collector's Value Guide™ to Ty® *Beanie Babies* answer the rest of your questions about the beloved collectibles. In its eighth edition, the book is bigger and better than ever! Inside you'll find color pictures of the entire *Beanie Babies* line, including the new August 31, 1999 releases, along with *Beanie Buddies*™ and *Teenie Beanie Babies*™ and the latest secondary market information. But the fun doesn't stop there! You'll learn how the line began and how these small, under-stuffed toys became a collecting phenomenon within months of being introduced.

Our Collector's Value Guide™ is a reference guide for collectors of all ages, designed to help you keep track of your collection, keep up with the constantly changing prices on the secondary market and gain insight into the different aspects of *Beanie Babies*, including:

 The Most Recent Releases And Retirements For *Beanie Babies* and *Beanie Buddies*

 The 10 Most Valuable *Beanie Babies*

 A *Beanie Babies* Timeline

 How To Shop The Secondary Market

 Beanie Babies In The News

 How To Tell If Your *Beanie Babies* Are Counterfeit

 And So Much More

THE INCREDIBLE BEANIE BABIES® STORY

Years ago, no one would have believed that a handful of beans would stir the passions of young and old alike and create an enduring phenomenon the likes of which had never been seen before! Yet this is exactly what Ty's *Beanie Babies* have managed to do. How did these bean bag animals become such an international craze? Here's a glance at the makings of this decade's greatest hit.

1993 — The year that started it all, in 1993 nine little animal-shaped beanbag toys called *Beanie Babies* were introduced at a Chicago area trade show by Ty Inc., an Illinois stuffed animal manufacturer.

1994 — Ty's retailer catalog showcased the "Original Nine" *Beanie Babies,* billing them as small in size (a handful of beans and stuffing) and small in price (a week's allowance) for the young collector (and the young at heart).

1995 — Ty Inc. retired its first *Beanie Babies:* "Humphrey," "Slither" and "Trap." Also this year, Ty's six "Teddy" bears, introduced in June 1994, did an "about face" and were redesigned with new features. Retired shortly thereafter, these "Teddies" became highly sought after on the secondary market.

1996 — In response to requests from collectors for accurate information, Ty Inc. introduced their official Internet web site: *www.ty.com.* By 1999, more than 3 billion people had visited the site.

One of the few interviews conducted with Ty Warner appeared in the October 21, 1996 issue of *Forbes* magazine.

During the interview, Ty commented on his company's policy to only sell his product line to small, independent gift stores. "This thing could grow and be around for many years," he said, "just as long as I don't take the easy road and sell it to a mass merchant who's going to put it in bins."

That fall, Warner gave each of his employees a special violet "Teddy." Only a very limited number of these new-faced, tag-less bears were produced, making it one of the most rare and sought after of all the *Beanies.*

1997 — "Quackers" became the first "Info Beanie" on the Ty web site to keep fans updated with new and noteworthy information. Writing in a diary format, he shared day-to-day information about the life of a *Beanie Baby* and occasionally provided hints about upcoming events and new releases. Collectors soon had the opportunity to vote for future "Info Beanies."

The first McDonald's Happy Meal toy giveaway in April made headlines when some restaurants ran out of *Teenie Beanie Babies* in only three days. The planned five-week promotion created a collector frenzy as fans lined up at drive-through windows to take home as many of the ten miniature *Beanie Baby* designs as possible.

In 1997, Ty Inc. also hit a home run by joining forces with the Chicago Cubs in May during the first *Beanie Babies* giveaway at a major sports event. Since then, more than 50 Major League Baseball promotions have been held, with other sports orga-nizations – the NBA, WNBA, NFL and NHL – eventually joining the *Beanie* team.

1998 — WH Smith opened the first "Tyriffic," an exclu-sive retail store at O'Hare International Airport in Chicago, which provided collectors with a great place to shop for Ty products and showcased samples of prototypes and rare *Beanie Babies*. Also, the Beanie Babies® Official Club™ was launched by Ty in conjunction with Cyrk Inc. in the spring of 1998. Membership included such perks as an exclusive *Beanie Babies* club bear named "Clubby."

"Valentino" became the only *Beanie Baby* to be "inducted" into the Baseball Hall of Fame in Cooperstown, New York. The Hall of Fame 1998 highlights exhibit commemorated Yankees pitcher David Wells' perfect game on May 17, and showcased Wells' cap, a ticket stub and "Valentino," the *Beanie Babies* giveaway at Yankees Stadium that day.

Also this year, Ty Warner gave each of his employees a special brown bear in September which featured a tag signed by Warner and a dollar sign on its chest. The bear was presented, according to the special inscription on the tag, "In recognition of value and contributions in shipping over a billion dollars since Jan '98 . . ." The special *Beanie's* name? "Billionaire Bear," of course!

1999 — The Ty Talk Cyberboard made its debut on the Ty web site. An overwhelming success, it was overloaded by collectors within hours of its introduction! After a temporary shutdown to expand its capacity, the board was reinstated and is now one of the most popular sections on the web site.

On August 31, 1999, the lights went out on the Ty web site, only to return with the announcement of 10 new *Beanie Babies* and 13 new *Beanie Buddies*. (New *Attic Treasures* and *Ty Plush* animals were introduced as well.) But the big news came when the company surprised the world with the notice that all Ty *Beanies* are scheduled to retire on December 31, 1999!

BEANIE BABIES® TIMELINE

Here's a look at some of the *Beanie Babies* highlights and "firsts" from 1993 through today:

1993 – The first nine *Beanie Babies* debut at a Chicago gift show.

1994 – "Mystic," the first imaginary creature is released.

June 15, 1995 – The first three *Beanie Babies* retire.

1996 – Ty Inc. unveils an official web site for *Beanie Baby* fans.

1996 – Birthdates and poems appear inside the *Beanie Baby* swing tags.

Doodle™ style 4171

DATE OF BIRTH : 3 - 8 - 96

Listen closely to "cock-a-doodle-doo"
What's the rooster saying to you?
Hurry, wake up sleepy head
We have lots to do, get out of bed!

Visit our web page!!!
http://www.ty.com

1997 – The first "Info *Beanie*" makes its debut on *www.ty.com*.

BEANIE BABIES® TIMELINE

April 11, 1997 — McDonald's introduces its first *Teenie Beanie Babies* promotion.

May 18, 1997 — The first sports promotion arrives with much fanfare.

Oct. 29, 1997 — "Princess," the first *Beanie Baby* to officially benefit a charity, is released.

1998 — The Beanie Babies Official Club, along with the special bear, "Clubby," debuts.

1999 — *Beanie Baby* tush tags with holograms appear to help deter counterfeits.

Millenium™
HANDMADE IN CHINA
© 1999 TY INC.,
OAKBROOK, IL. U.S.A.
SURFACE WASHABLE
ALL NEW MATERIAL
POLYESTER FIBER
& P.E. PELLETS
REG.NO PA.1965(KR)

Aug. 31, 1999 — Ty Inc. announces all Ty *Beanies* are scheduled to retire on December 31, 1999.

BEANIE BABIES®
IN THE NEWS

Beanie Babies are not only a favorite among collectors, but they are sure-fire headline news throughout the world. Here's a peek at some recent news stories:

AND THE WINNER IS

During the Miss Teen U.S.A. 1999 pageant, Miss Delaware talked about her collection of 115 *Beanie Babies.* When asked which *Beanie* she would give away if she had to, 18-year-old Ashley Coleman selected "Hope" – to share its message of hope with others.

CHARITY BEGINS AT HOME

This summer, Ty Inc. generously donated $1 million to the Ronald McDonald House Charities®. The charity helps support more than 200 Ronald McDonald Houses around the world that offer families of sick children a place to stay during their child's hospitalization.

ONLY A DOZEN, PLEASE

Ty Inc. has authorized the U.S. Customs Service to allow overseas travelers to bring home up to 12 *Beanie Babies* per person. Included in the regulations is the restriction that no more than three of each animal are allowed through Customs. *Beanie Babies* purchased in China, South Korea or Indonesia, however, are not allowed into the United States at all, as there are no licensed Ty distributors in those countries, therefore items bought in those countries are either counterfeit or stolen.

BEANIE BABIES® IN THE NEWS

TY® TAKES TOKYO

Ty made its web site available in both Japanese and German languages in September 1999 and there were reports of *Beanie Babies* being sold in some Japanese retail/toy stores. An article in the *Washington Post* on August 19, 1999 documented the arrival of the popular toys in the land where "Pokémon" originated.

THE GREAT BLACKOUT

Ty forewarned us that an important announcement would appear on the official Ty web site on August 31, but collectors were surprised when, at midnight, the home page became a black screen. A brief news flash in mid-afternoon finally introduced new *Beanie Babies, Beanie Buddies, Attic Treasures* and *Ty Plush.* But the news was tempered with the surprising and cryptic message: all Ty *Beanies* are scheduled to retire December 31, 1999. Although the announcement disappeared from the Ty web site shortly thereafter, its message made front-page news around the world.

THE REAL THING

Nurses at the neonatal unit at Connecticut Children's Medical Center are concerned about the possible retirement of all *Beanies.* They use the toys to add a bit of comfort to their tiny patients, according to a September 4, 1999 article in *The Hartford Courant.* "When a 2-pound newborn is sleeping, a Dalmatian might be propped between the baby's legs to keep the hips aligned. A cow, strategically placed on the chest, can calm a crying baby." News of an impending retirement is worrisome because, as the article says, "Cheap imitations, it seems, are just not the same."

SPOTLIGHT ON THE NEW RELEASES

The summer of 1999 has held many surprises for *Beanie* collectors. Three special *Beanie Babies* releases – "B.B. Bear" the bear, "Flitter" the butterfly and "Lips" the fish – made their debut at the Dallas Gift Show on June 26 where they could be viewed for the first time and retailers could place orders. The following month, two new *Beanie Buddies* were announced on the Ty web site: "Inch" the worm and "Schweetheart" the orangutan.

The biggest surprise came with the August 31 announcement of 10 new *Beanie Babies* and 13 new *Beanie Buddies*, along with news that all Ty *Beanies* are scheduled to be retired on December 31, 1999!

HERE'S A LOOK AT THE NEW BEANIE BABIES®:

Looking forward to the holidays, "1999 Holiday Teddy" is prepared for the chill in the air and ready to warm your heart. His powder-blue fur is sprinkled all over with white snowflakes, flurrying with the excitement of the season.

"B.B. Bear" is sure to be one of the most celebrated bears released by Ty. This pastel tie-dyed bear aims to make sure that all your dreams-come-true!

"Chipper" is on the lookout for nuts to store in his food collection for those long cold winter days ahead. He hopes that you'll want to store him in your *Beanie* collection.

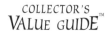

Spotlight On The New Releases

"**Flitter**" fluttered into the collection this summer at the Dallas Gift Show. She shows off her wings in pastel shades of blues, pinks and greens which complement her stunning pink body.

The fur is tie-dyed and the nose is purple, so it isn't surprising that this bear's name is "**Groovy**." This trendy teddy has a flair for retro, so dig out your bell-bottoms and put your favorite Beatles record on the turntable!

The day before his friend "Loosy" was retired, "**Honks**" arrived at the Ty lake. He will soon be flying south for the winter himself so act fast and catch him as he flies through your town on his way down!

Named for its best feature, "**Lips**" came swimming in this summer, and camouflage is the last thing on its mind! This colorful critter is the newest fish in the Ty tank of fun!

After his reptilian relative "Lizzy" retired in 1997, "**Scaly**" has crawled into the Ty lizard family. He's so excited to meet *Beanie Babies* collectors that he's proudly showing off his own reptilian colors and the only thing he'll never shed is his love for you.

COLLECTOR'S
VALUE GUIDE™

A sloth with a smile! "Slowpoke" got tired of just sitting around and decided to join in the fun! Watch for him as he swings into the Ty family tree.

Floating in for Halloween, "Sheets" puts on a scary face to keep the shivers in his favorite holiday! But it's hard to be scary when you're so cute! Pick him up before he follows "Spooky" into the Ty retirement graveyard!

Commemorating the end of the millennium and the retirement of his friends, "The End" celebrates the end of an era with the explosion of fireworks on his chest and watches as his *Beanie* pals go out with a bang!

"Ty 2K" looks like he got caught in a flurry of falling confetti! His white fur is color-fully splattered, and he is ready to celebrate the advent of the new year. And there are no bugs here – only hugs!

Straight from the Scottish Highlands, with a red plaid scarf and a rich forest green coat, "Wallace" will place high in your heart!

A BEAR IN EVERY BASKET!

On September 12, 1999, news of a tiny bear invaded the annual Ty family picnic. It was announced that "Billionaire #2" would be given to each Ty employee in celebration of another successful year for the company.

HERE'S A LOOK AT THE NEW BEANIE BUDDIES® :

Almost larger than real life, this gold striped tabby *Buddy* will be a favorite among the feline fanatics! "Amber" will keep her nose clean and be sure to claw her way into your heart!

Proudly wearing the Union Jack flag on her chest, **"Britannia"** the *Buddy* bear is a U.K. exclusive, just like her *Beanie Babies* namesake.

For dog lovers, this large *Buddy* version of the *Beanie Baby* golden retriever will be the catch of the day when you bring him home. Loyal and true, "Fetch" will put a smile on your face and will be your friend forever!

While **"Clubby"** the *Beanie Baby* became "larger than life" as the first Beanie Babies Official Club piece, its larger namesake is even bigger. The teddy is available only to Gold Club members.

But both Gold and Platinum Club Members have the opportunity to purchase "Clubby II." With his soft fur, this *Buddy* will be an irresistible find!

"Gobbles" the turkey will steal the show at your Thanksgiving get-together! She's the center of attention wherever she is – posing in the center of the dining table or greeting guests at the door!

The extremely popular angel *Beanie Baby* now has a big sister! With a halo over her head and wings on her back, **"Halo"** can be the guardian of everyone in need of a little love and care!

It may have taken him a bit longer than he expected, but **"Inch"** has finally wormed his way in to join the rest of the *Beanie Buddies*. "Inch" may be slow but you sure won't be able to overlook him as his brilliant colors rush into your heart!

This snow-white bear that honors our neighbor to the north proudly bears the red maple design of his country's flag on his chest. A Canadian exclusive, **"Maple"** the *Beanie Buddy* joins the growing roster of Ty's popular international bears.

Although this colorful *Buddy* of tie-dye design is reminiscent of the 1960s and '70s, **"Peace"** carries his timeless, international message to all people – make peace, not war!

"Pumkin'" the *Beanie Buddy* wants to come along for all the trick-or-treating at your house! And who can resist his happy gap-toothed smile and those long green arms made just for hugging?

Spotlight On The New Releases

For the wild at heart, **"Schweetheart"** the lovable orangutan is the perfect addition for your *Beanie Buddy* collection. His arms are ready for a squeeze before he swings up to the trees!

"Silver" bounds in with love in her heart and a swish in her tail – and makes a perfect companion for her best buddy, "Amber." What a pair they would make sitting in a basket of yarn!

Every animal needs a friend in the trees! **"Slither"** snakes his way in to play with his buddies for a very "vine" day in the jungle!

A very special *Buddy* indeed, "Snowboy" stands on his own merit without a companion *Beanie Baby* of the same design. All bundled up for winter, he seems to have forgotten to keep his nose warm – it has turned a bright cherry red!

"Spangle" is the *Buddy* bear with the American flair! Sporting stripes and stars of red, white and blue, "Spangle" is proud to represent her country with her friends "Maple" and "Britannia."

What's the perfect spot for this spider with a LARGE attitude? Why, on top of your computer, of course! **"Spinner"** will feel right at home near the "web" at either your home or office.

COLLECTOR'S
VALUE GUIDE™

18

COLLECTOR'S CLUB NEWS

Ty Inc. delighted *Beanie Babies* fans in the spring of 1998 when it created the Beanie Babies® Official Club™ (BBOC™) in conjunction with the promotions company Cyrk Inc. In addition to the original BBOC Gold Kit, members were able to purchase the club's first members only *Beanie Baby,* "Clubby." Then, in 1999, the BBOC issued its Platinum Kit with "Clubby II" and several other fun items.

A benefit of becoming a member of the BBOC is the opportunity to purchase exclusive members' pieces. The first special pieces are the *Beanie Buddy* bears "Clubby" and "Clubby II," which were made available for purchase for a limited time. As a bonus for those who hold both Gold and Platinum Cards, four *Beanie Baby/Buddy* Collector Cards will be shipped with every *Buddy* order.

Made available to only BBOC Gold Card holders, "Clubby" the *Beanie Buddy* is outfitted in luxurious blue fur and sports a tie-dyed neck ribbon and a BBOC patch over his heart. He is one *Buddy* that will hold a special place in your heart and a special spot on your shelf.

"Clubby II," the *Beanie Buddy*, became available to any BBOC member who holds either a Platinum or a Gold Card. This *Buddy* is dressed in luscious lavender fur, wears a neck ribbon and is a "must-have" for club members.

Club members may order the exclusive *Beanie Buddies* by credit card through the Beanie Babies Official Club web site (*www.beaniebabyofficialclub.com*) or by calling 1-888-750-1101.

THE WONDERFUL WORLD OF TY®

Most people automatically think of *Beanie Babies* when they hear the word "Ty," but Ty Inc. has been around twice as long as its famous beanbag animals. The company's first line of stuffed animals, *Ty Plush*, came out in 1986, followed by *Attic Treasures*™ in 1993, *Beanie Babies* in 1994, *Pillow Pals*™ in 1995, *Teenie Beanie Babies* in 1997 and *Beanie Buddies* in 1998.

TY® PLUSH

In 1986, a litter of cats and a few dogs called *Ty Plush* entered the stuffed animal world. Owners of pieces from this original group now possess some valuable plush animals! Over the years, additional animals were released in this line in the following groups: Bears, Cats, Dogs, Country and Wildlife. The 361 pieces in the *Ty Plush* collection now include a variety of animals, from lions and tigers and bears to puppies and kittens and bunnies.

ATTIC TREASURES™

Ty introduced a group of adorable bears and rabbits to the world in 1993 with fully-jointed arms and legs so they could be positioned to show any position in life. The original *Attic Treasures* came without clothes, often donning ribbons, but during 1996, many of the animals began sporting such clothing as jumpers.

There are now 140 animals in the collection – which includes dogs, cats, frogs, a hippo and even a monkey or two – and most of the newer pieces are clothed.

Originally called *The Attic Treasures Collection*, the line's name was changed to "Ty Collectibles" shortly after its release. In 1998, the collection reverted to its original name.

PILLOW PALS™

Introduced in 1995, *Pillow Pals* were specifically designed for infants. Made of soft plush materials, the animals' features are embroidered eyes and sewn-on ribbons.

Pillow Pals originally came in soft pastel colors – perfect for little boys and girls. But in 1999, the animals began sporting a palette of vivid colors to catch infants' eyes. To date, a total of 43 *Pillow Pals* have been released.

TEENIE BEANIE BABIES™

Ty Inc. teamed up with McDonald's in 1997 for a promotion that included ten smaller versions of *Beanie Babies*. After three promotions over the last three years, there are now a total of 38 *Teenie Beanie Babies*.

BEANIE BUDDIES™

When the popularity of *Beanie Babies* was reaching its all-time high, Ty Inc. introduced yet another line of animals. In 1998, *Beanie Buddies* made their debut. These bigger versions of *Beanie Babies* are made with a soft fur called Tylon®. So far, there are 45 *Beanie Buddies*, including the club specials.

FAREWELL TO THE BEANIES™

With the arrival of the new millennium comes the end of the *Beanie* phenomenon as we know it. Fifteen *Beanie Babies* and two *Beanie Buddies* have recently retired, and a mysterious Ty newsflash at the end of August has the entire world wondering whether this be the end of the *Beanies*. We'll have to wait and see! For now, here's an update on the recent *Beanie Babies* and *Beanie Buddies* retirements.

BEANIE BABIES®

RETIRED 9/1/99
Loosy™ (goose, #4206, 1998)

RETIRED 8/27/99
Wiser™ (owl, #4238, 1999)

RETIRED 8/24/99
Fortune™ (panda, #4196, 1998)

RETIRED 8/16/99
Canyon™ (cougar, #4212, 1998)

RETIRED 7/28/99
Eggbert™ (chick, #4232, 1999)

RETIRED 7/26/99
Britannia™ (bear, #4601, 1997)

RETIRED 7/20/99
Nibbly™ (rabbit, #4217, 1999)

RETIRED 7/19/99
Ewey™ (lamb, #4219, 1999)

RETIRED 7/14/99
Peace™ (bear, #4053, 1997)

RETIRED 7/12/99
Hippie™ (bunny, #4218, 1999)

RETIRED 7/9/99
Nibbler™ (rabbit, #4216, 1999)

RETIRED 5/31/99
Stilts™ (stork, #4221, 1999)

RETIRED 5/26/99
Derby™ (horse, #4008, 1995)

RETIRED 5/21/99
Erin™ (bear, #4186, 1998)

RETIRED 5/18/99
Mystic™ (unicorn, #4007, 1994)

BEANIE BUDDIES™

RETIRED 7/27/99
Patti™ (platypus, #9320, 1999)

RETIRED 7/21/99
Quackers™ (duck, #9302, 1998)

Ty Newsflash!
August 31, 1999

<u>VERY IMPORTANT NOTICE:</u>
On December 31, 1999 –
11:59 p.m. (CST)
All Beanies will be retired . . .

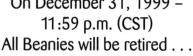

BEANIE BABIES® TOP TEN

Beanie Babies continue to be a hot item on the secondary market. And while many of them stay close to their original price, some of them soar in value. This "Top Ten" list is dedicated to those *Beanies* whose values remain strong and keep collectors on a personal *Beanie Baby* hunt. The majority of the most valuable *Beanies* are rare, limited pieces or were introduced early in the *Beanie* days with older generation swing tags. It's important to note that because the secondary market often changes, so may the price.

#1 Bear™
Bear, Ty Sales Rep Gift
Market Value: Special Tag – $10,800

Peanut™
Elephant, Dark Blue Version
Market Value: ❸ – $4,700

Nana™
Monkey
Market Value: ❸ – $4,000

Teddy™ (violet)
Bear, Ty Employee Gift
Market Value: No Swing Tag – $3,800

Pinchers™
Lobster, "Punchers™" Swing Tag Version
Market Value:  – $3,400

Brownie™
Bear
Market Value: – $3,350

Billionaire Bear™
Bear, Ty Employee Gift
Market Value: Special Tag – $3,300

Derby™
Horse, No Star/Fine Mane Version
Market Value: – $3,100

Teddy™ (brown)
Bear, Old Face Version
Market Value: – $2,600

Humphrey™
Camel
Market Value: – $2,400

How To Use Your Collector's Value Guide™

There are four simple steps in determining the current market value of your collection:

1 **Record** the price paid and the date purchased for each *Beanie Baby* you own in the allotted space.

2 **Use** the swing tag generation chart on the right to help identify your *Beanie Baby* tag generation (for more information on tag generations, see pages 165-169).

SWING TAG KEY

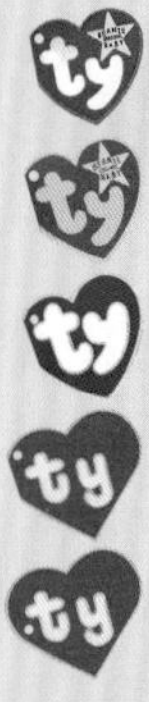

- 5 – 5th Generation
- 4 – 4th Generation
- 3 – 3rd Generation
- 2 – 2nd Generation
- 1 – 1st Generation

3 **Find** the value of the piece by looking at the dollar amount listed next to the corresponding heart. For current *Beanie Babies* with a fifth generation tag, fill in the current market value, which is usually the price you paid. If a piece's value is not established, it is listed as "N/E." *Sports Promotion Beanie Babies* are listed beginning on page 138 and are marked in the Value Guide with the appropriate symbol. *Beanie Buddies* begin on page 142, while the *Teenie Beanie Babies* section begins on page 154.

SPORTS PROMOTION BEANIE BABIES® KEY

- Canadian Special Olympics
- Major League Baseball
- National Basketball Association
- National Football League
- National Hockey League
- Women's National Basketball Association

4 **Add** the "Market Value" for each *Beanie Baby* you own and write the sum in the "Value Totals" box at the bottom of each page. Use a pencil so you can make changes as your collection grows. Write in your totals from each Value Guide page on pages 161-162 and add the sums together to get the "Grand Total" of your Ty collection.

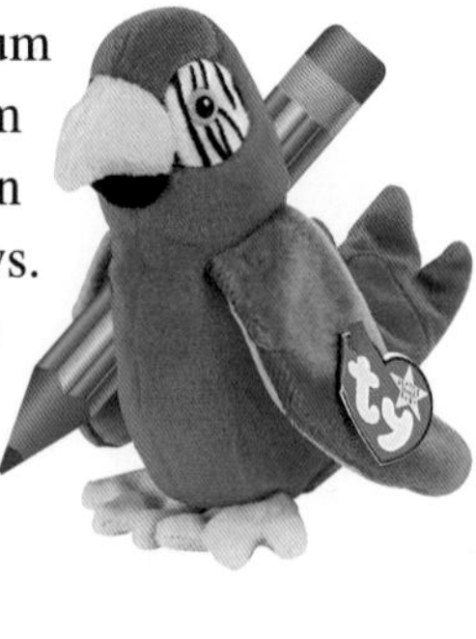

Let's Party Like It's 1999!

Ty Inc.'s *Beanie Babies* have become an indelible part of the 20th century's final decade. Their introduction in 1994 has caused an unexpected surge in the toy collectibles market, a trend that is sure to continue into the new millennium. This section provides you with information on all 220 *Beanie Babies* released to date, including issue and retirement dates, poems, birthdates and secondary market values for each tag generation. Current Beanies are rated according to the "degree of difficulty".of finding them in retail stores.

DEGREE OF DIFFICULTY RATINGS

Just Released	*Hard To Find*
Easy To Find	*Very Hard To Find*
Moderate To Find	*Impossible To Find*

#1 Bear™
(exclusive Ty sales
representative gift)

Bear · N/A
Issued: December 12, 1998
Not Available In
Retail Stores

Market Value:
Special Tag – $10,800

Dedication Appearing On Special Tag
In appreciation of selling over several Billion
dollars in 1998 and achieving the industry
ranking of #1 in Gift sales, #1 in
Collectible sales, #1 in Cash register area
sales, #1 in Markup %, I present to you
This Signed and Numbered bear!

Birthdate: N/A
Price Paid: $_____
Date Purchased: _____
Tag Generation: _____

2

1997
Teddy™

Bear · #4200
Issued: October 1, 1997
Retired: December 31, 1997

Market Value:
➍-$57

Beanie Babies are special no doubt
All filled with love – inside and out
Wishes for fun times filled with joy
Ty's holiday teddy is a magical toy!

Birthdate: December 25, 1996
Price Paid: $_____
Date Purchased: _____
Tag Generation: _____

3

1998
Holiday Teddy™

Bear · #4204
Issued: September 30, 1998
Retired: December 31, 1998

Market Value:
➎-$60

Dressed in his PJ's, and ready for bed
Hugs given, good nights said
This little Beanie will stay close at night
Ready for a hug at first morning light!

Birthdate: December 25, 1998
Price Paid: $_____
Date Purchased: _____
Tag Generation: _____

Value
Totals: _____

COLLECTOR'S
VALUE GUIDE™

4

1999 Holiday Teddy™

Bear · #4257
Issued: August 31, 1999
Current - Just Released

Market Value:
[5]- $_____

NEW!

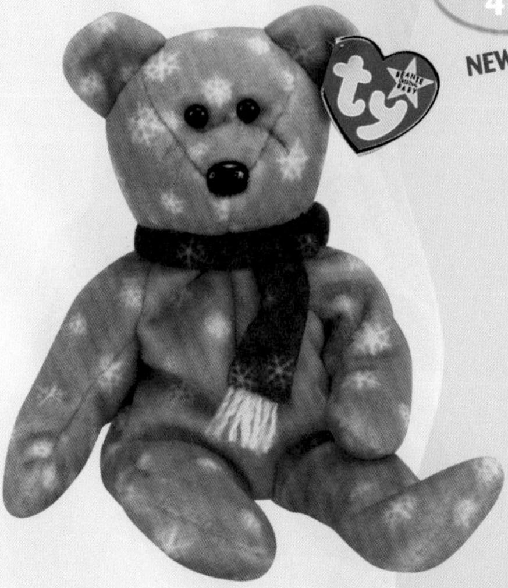

Birthdate: December 25, 1999
Price Paid: $__________
Date Purchased: __________
Tag Generation: __________

Peace on Earth as the holidays grow near
The season is all about giving good cheer
With love and joy in your hearts
Lets all be friends as the century starts!

5

1999 Signature Bear™

Bear · #4228
Issued: January 1, 1999
Current - Moderate To Find

Market Value:
[5]- $_____

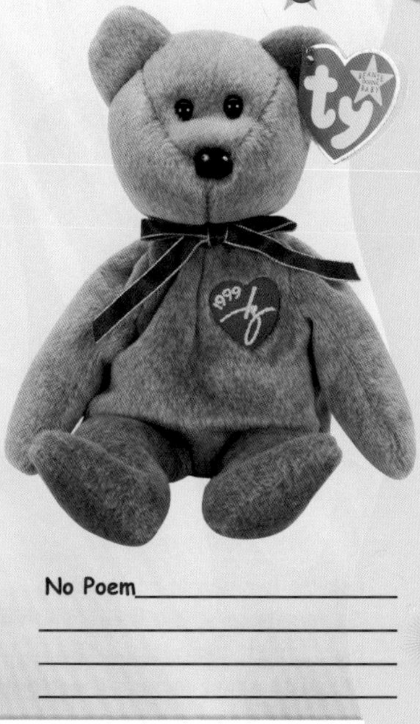

Birthdate: N/A
Price Paid: $__________
Date Purchased: __________
Tag Generation: __________

No Poem

COLLECTOR'S VALUE GUIDE™

Value Totals: __________

6

Ally™

Alligator · #4032
Issued: June 25, 1994
Retired: October 1, 1997

Market Value:
4 – $55
3 – $125
2 – $270
1 – $425

When Ally gets out of classes
He wears a hat and dark glasses
He plays bass in a street band
He's the coolest gator in the land!

Birthdate: March 14, 1994
Price Paid: $_____
Date Purchased: _____
Tag Generation: _____

7

Almond™

Bear · #4246
Issued: April 19, 1999
Current – Moderate To Find

Market Value:
5 – $_____

Leaving her den in early spring
So very hungry, she'll eat anything
Nuts, fruit, berries and fish
Mixed together make a great dish!

Birthdate: April 14, 1999
Price Paid: $_____
Date Purchased: _____
Tag Generation: _____

Value
Totals: _____

COLLECTOR'S
VALUE GUIDE™

Amber™

8

Cat • #4243
Issued: April 20, 1999
Current – Moderate To Find

Market Value:
🖐-$_____

Birthdate: February 21, 1999
Price Paid: $_____
Date Purchased: _____
Tag Generation: _____

Sleeping all day and up all night
Waiting to pounce and give you a fright
She means no harm, just playing a game
She's very lovable and quite tame!

Ants™

9

Anteater • #4195
Issued: May 30, 1998
Retired: December 31, 1998

Market Value:
🖐-$12

Birthdate: November 7, 1997
Price Paid: $_____
Date Purchased: _____
Tag Generation: _____

Most anteaters love to eat bugs
But this little fellow gives big hugs
He'd rather dine on apple pie
Than eat an ant or harm a fly!

COLLECTOR'S
VALUE GUIDE™

10

NEW!

B.B. Bear™

Bear · #4253
Issued: Summer 1999
Current – Just Released

Market Value:
❺- $_____

This birthday Beanie was made for you
Hope your wishes and dreams come true
Be happy today and tomorrow too
Let's all celebrate the whole year through!

Birthdate: N/A
Price Paid: $_____
Date Purchased: _____
Tag Generation: _____

11

Baldy™

Eagle · #4074
Issued: May 11, 1997
Retired: May 1, 1998

Market Value:
❺- $18
❹- $23

Hair on his head is quite scant
We suggest Baldy get a transplant
Watching over the land of the free
Hair in his eyes would make it hard to see!

Birthdate: February 17, 1996
Price Paid: $_____
Date Purchased: _____
Tag Generation: _____

Value
Totals: _____

COLLECTOR'S
VALUE GUIDE™

Batty™

12

Bat · #4035
Issued: October 1, 1997
Retired: March 31, 1999

Market Value:
A. Tie-dye
(Jan. 99-March 99)
[5]-$23
B. Brown
(Est. Oct. 97-Jan. 99)
[5]-$15
[4]-$19

A

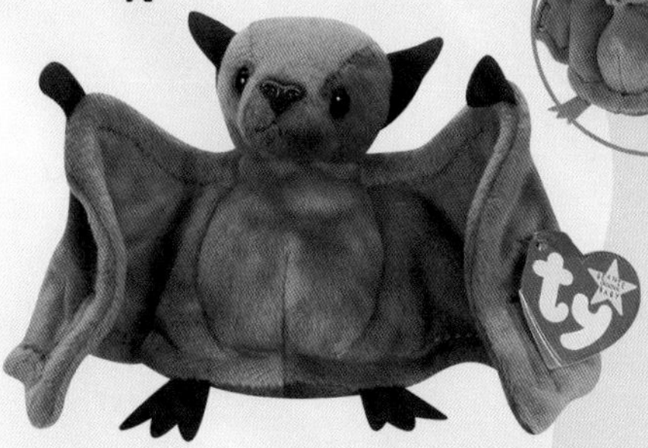

B

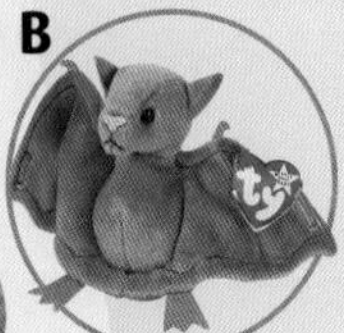

Birthdate: October 29, 1996
Price Paid: $__________
Date Purchased: __________
Tag Generation: __________

Bats may make some people jitter
Please don't be scared of this critter
If you're lonely or have nothing to do
This Beanie Baby would love to hug you!

Beak™

13

Kiwi · #4211
Current - Easy To Find

Market Value:
[5]-$_____

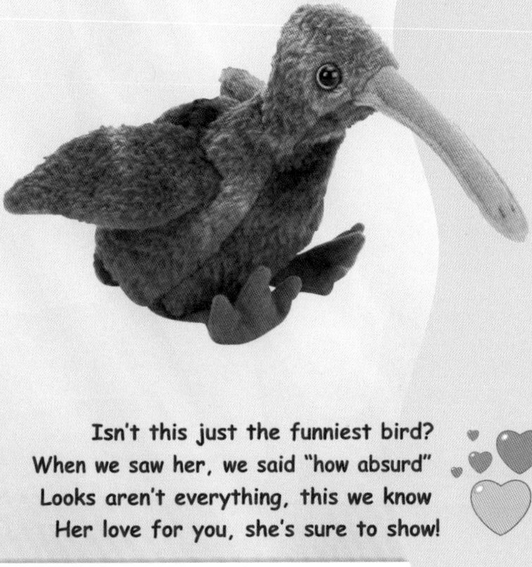

Birthdate: February 3, 1998
Price Paid: $__________
Date Purchased: __________
Tag Generation: __________

Isn't this just the funniest bird?
When we saw her, we said "how absurd"
Looks aren't everything, this we know
Her love for you, she's sure to show!

Value Totals: __________

14

Bernie™

St. Bernard · #4109
Issued: January 1, 1997
Retired: September 22, 1998

Market Value:
[5]-$12
[4]-$15

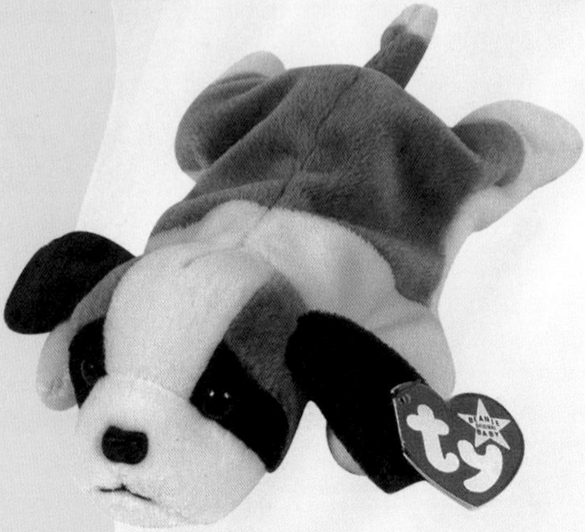

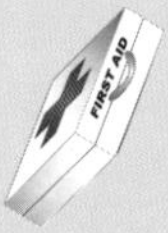

This little dog can't wait to grow
To rescue people lost in the snow
Don't let him out - keep him on your shelf
He doesn't know how to rescue himself!

Birthdate: October 3, 1996
Price Paid: $__________
Date Purchased: __________
Tag Generation: __________

15

Bessie™

Cow · #4009
Issued: June 3, 1995
Retired: October 1, 1997

Market Value:
[4]-$70
[3]-$135

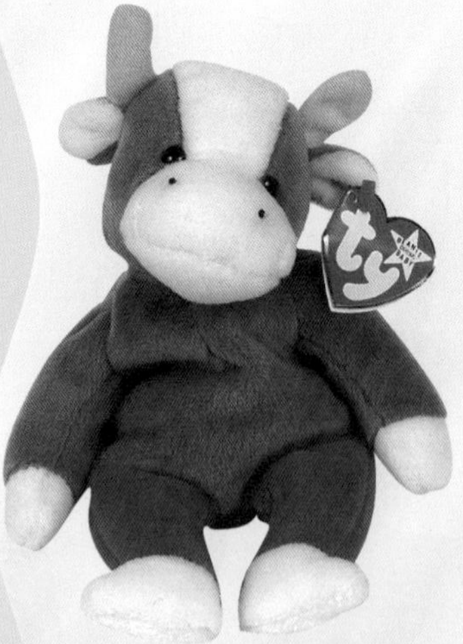

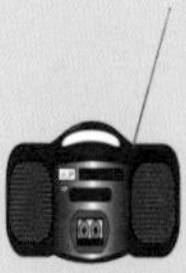

Bessie the cow likes to dance and sing
Because music is her favorite thing
Every night when you are counting sheep
She'll sing you a song to help you sleep!

Birthdate: June 27, 1995
Price Paid: $__________
Date Purchased: __________
Tag Generation: __________

Value Totals: __________

16

Billionaire Bear™

(exclusive Ty employee gift)

Bear • N/A
Issued: September 26, 1998
Not Available In
Retail Stores

Market Value:
Special Tag – $3,300

Birthdate: N/A
Price Paid: $_____
Date Purchased: _____
Tag Generation: _____

Dedication Appearing On Special Tag
In recognition of value and
contributions in shipping over
a billion dollars since Jan '98,
I present to you this exclusive signed bear!

17

NEW!

Billionaire™ #2

(exclusive Ty employee gift)

Bear • N/A
Issued: September 12, 1999
Not Available In
Retail Stores

Market Value:
Special Tag – N/E

Birthdate: N/A
Price Paid: $_____
Date Purchased: _____
Tag Generation: _____

Tag Information Unavailable
_____
_____
_____
_____

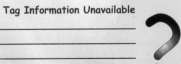

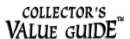

18

Blackie™

Bear · #4011
Issued: June 25, 1994
Retired: September 15, 1998

Market Value:
5- $16
4- $18
3- $100
2- $235
1- $340

Living in a national park
He only played after dark
Then he met his friend Cubbie
Now they play when it's sunny!

Birthdate: July 15, 1994
Price Paid: $_____
Date Purchased: _____
Tag Generation: _____

19

Blizzard™

Tiger · #4163
Issued: May 11, 1997
Retired: May 1, 1998

Market Value:
5- $22
4- $26

In the mountains, where it's snowy and cold
Lives a beautiful tiger, I've been told
Black and white, she's hard to compare
Of all the tigers, she is most rare!

Birthdate: December 12, 1996
Price Paid: $_____
Date Purchased: _____
Tag Generation: _____

Value
Totals: _____

COLLECTOR'S
VALUE GUIDE™

Bones™

20

Dog · #4001
Issued: June 25, 1994
Retired: May 1, 1998

Market Value:
- ❺-$18
- ❹-$20
- ❸-$100
- ❷-$230
- ❶-$320

Birthdate: January 18, 1994
Price Paid: $_____
Date Purchased: _____
Tag Generation: _____

Bones is a dog that loves to chew
Chairs and tables and a smelly old shoe
"You're so destructive" all would shout
But that all stopped, when his teeth
Fell out!

Bongo™
(name changed from "Nana™")

21

A

Monkey · #4067
Issued: June 3, 1995
Retired: December 31, 1998

Market Value:
A. Tan Tail
   (June 95-Dec. 98)
- ❺-$13
- ❹-$15
- ❸-$165
B. Brown Tail
   (Feb. 96–June 96)
- ❹-$60
- ❸-$155

B

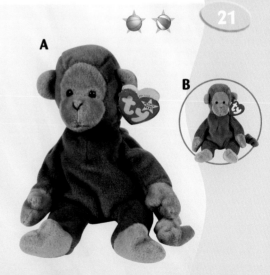

Birthdate: August 17, 1995
Price Paid: $_____
Date Purchased: _____
Tag Generation: _____

Bongo the monkey lives in a tree
The happiest monkey you'll ever see
In his spare time he plays the guitar
One of these days he will be a big star!

22

Britannia™

(exclusive to the United Kingdom)

Bear · #4601
Issued: December 31, 1997
Retired: July 26, 1999

Market Value:
[5]- $165

Britannia the bear will sail the sea
So she can be with you and me
She's always sure to catch the tide
And wear the Union Flag with pride

Birthdate: December 15, 1997
Price Paid: $__________
Date Purchased: __________
Tag Generation: __________

23

Bronty™

Brontosaurus · #4085
Issued: June 3, 1995
Retired: June 15, 1996

Market Value:
[3]- $900

No Poem__________________
____
____
____

Birthdate: N/A
Price Paid: $__________
Date Purchased: __________
Tag Generation: __________

Value Totals: __________

Brownie™
(name changed to "Cubbie™")

Bear • #4010
Issued: January 8, 1994
Retired: 1994

Market Value:
❶-$3,350

Birthdate: N/A
Price Paid: $_____
Date Purchased: _____
Tag Generation: _____

No Poem_____
_____
_____
_____

Bruno™

Dog • #4183
Issued: December 31, 1997
Retired: September 18, 1998

Market Value:
❺-$12

Birthdate: September 9, 1997
Price Paid: $_____
Date Purchased: _____
Tag Generation: _____

Bruno the dog thinks he's a brute
But all the other Beanies think he's cute
He growls at his tail and runs in a ring
And everyone says, "Oh, how darling!"

26

Bubbles™

Fish · #4078
Issued: June 3, 1995
Retired: May 11, 1997

Market Value:
❹- $145
❸- $210

All day long Bubbles likes to swim
She never gets tired of flapping her fins
Bubbles lived in a sea of blue
Now she is ready to come home with you!

Birthdate: July 2, 1995
Price Paid: $_____
Date Purchased: _____
Tag Generation: _____

27

Bucky™

Beaver · #4016
Issued: January 7, 1996
Retired: December 31, 1997

Market Value:
❹- $35
❸- $105

Bucky's teeth are as shiny as can be
Often used for cutting trees
He hides in his dam night and day
Maybe for you he will come out and play!

Birthdate: June 8, 1995
Price Paid: $_____
Date Purchased: _____
Tag Generation: _____

Value
Totals: _____

COLLECTOR'S
VALUE GUIDE™

28

Bumble™

Bee · #4045
Issued: June 3, 1995
Retired: June 15, 1996

Market Value:
[4]-$575
[3]-$550

Birthdate: October 16, 1995
Price Paid: $__________
Date Purchased: __________
Tag Generation: __________

Bumble the bee will not sting you
It is only love that this bee will bring you
So don't be afraid to give this bee a hug
Because Bumble the bee is a love-bug.

29

Butch™

Bull Terrier · #4227
Issued: January 1, 1999
Current - Easy To Find

Market Value:
[5]-$_____

Birthdate: October 2, 1998
Price Paid: $__________
Date Purchased: __________
Tag Generation: __________

Going to the pet shop to buy dog food
I ran into Butch in a good mood
"Come to the pet shop down the street"
"Be a good dog, I'll buy you a treat!"

Value Totals: __________

30

Canyon™

Cougar · #4212
Issued: September 30, 1998
Retired: August 16, 1999

Market Value:
[5]-$_____

I climb rocks and really run fast
Try to catch me, it's a blast
Through the mountains, I used to roam
Now in your room, I'll call it home!

Birthdate: May 29, 1998
Price Paid: $__________
Date Purchased: __________
Tag Generation: __________

31

Caw™

Crow · #4071
Issued: June 3, 1995
Retired: June 15, 1996

Market Value:
[3]-$610

No Poem

Birthdate: N/A
Price Paid: $__________
Date Purchased: __________
Tag Generation: __________

Value Totals: __________

32

Cheeks™

Baboon · #4250
Issued: April 17, 1999
Current – Moderate To Find

Market Value:
[5]-$_____

Birthdate: May 18, 1999
Price Paid: $__________
Date Purchased: __________
Tag Generation: __________

Don't confuse me with an ape
I have a most unusual shape
My cheeks are round and ty-dyed red
On my behind as well as my head!

33

Chilly™

Polar Bear · #4012
Issued: June 25, 1994
Retired: January 7, 1996

Market Value:
[3]-$1,850
[2]-$2,000
[1]-$2,200

Birthdate: N/A
Price Paid: $__________
Date Purchased: __________
Tag Generation: __________

No Poem__________

34

Chip™

Cat · #4121
Issued: May 11, 1997
Retired: March 31, 1999

Market Value:
[5]- $11
[4]- $14

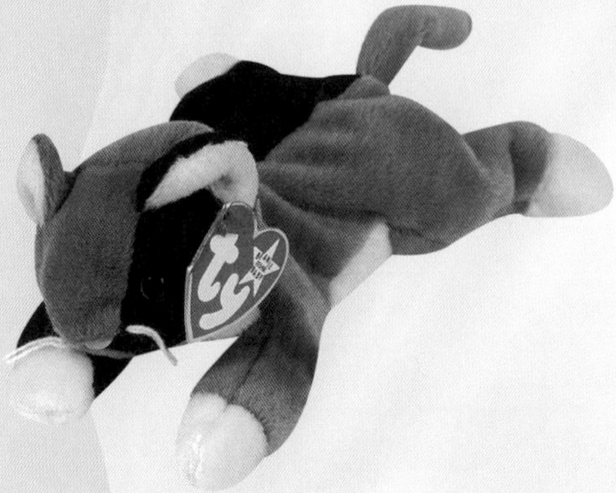

Black and gold, brown and white
The shades of her coat are quite a sight
At mixing her colors she was a master
On anyone else it would be a disaster!

Birthdate: January 26, 1996
Price Paid: $__________
Date Purchased: __________
Tag Generation: __________

35

NEW!

Chipper™

Chipmunk · #4259
Issued: August 31, 1999
Current – Just Released

Market Value:
[5]- $_____

I'm quick, I'm fast, I don't make a peep
But I love to snuggle when I sleep
Take me along when you go play
And I'll make sure you have a nice day!

Birthdate: April 21, 1999
Price Paid: $__________
Date Purchased: __________
Tag Generation: __________

Value Totals: __________

Chocolate™

36

Moose · #4015
Issued: January 8, 1994
Retired: December 31, 1998

Market Value:
[5] - $12
[4] - $15
[3] - $125
[2] - $320
[1] - $500

ORIGINAL NINE

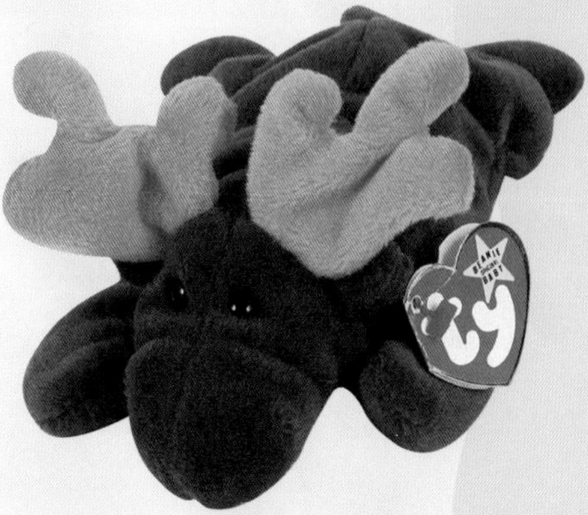

Birthdate: April 27, 1993
Price Paid: $__________
Date Purchased: __________
Tag Generation: __________

Licorice, gum and peppermint candy
This moose always has these handy
There is one more thing he likes to eat
Can you guess his favorite sweet?

Chops™

37

Lamb · #4019
Issued: January 7, 1996
Retired: January 1, 1997

Market Value:
[4] - $165
[3] - $230

Birthdate: May 3, 1996
Price Paid: $__________
Date Purchased: __________
Tag Generation: __________

Chops is a little lamb
This lamb you'll surely know
Because every path that you may take
This lamb is sure to go!

Value Totals: __________

38

Claude™

Crab · #4083
Issued: May 11, 1997
Retired: December 31, 1998

Market Value:
[5]- $14
[4]- $18

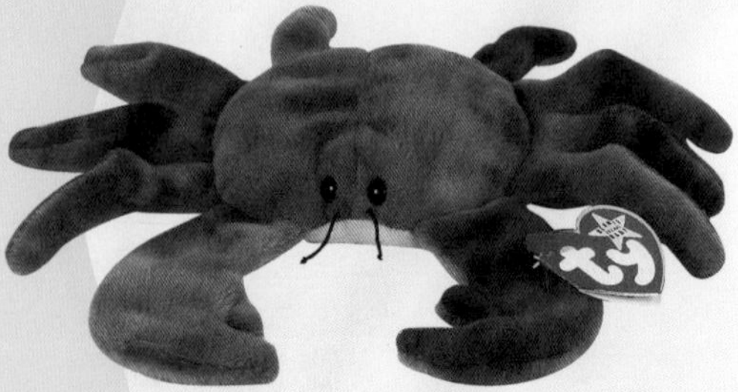

Claude the crab paints by the sea
A famous artist he hopes to be
But the tide came in and his paints fell
Now his art is on his shell!

Birthdate: September 3, 1996
Price Paid: $__________
Date Purchased: __________
Tag Generation: __________

39

Clubby™

(exclusive to Beanie Babies® Official Club™ members)

Bear · N/A
Issued: May 1, 1998
Retired: March 15, 1999

Market Value:
[5]- $45

Wearing his club pin for all to see
He's a proud member like you and me
Made especially with you in mind
Clubby the bear is one of a kind!

Birthdate: July 7, 1998
Price Paid: $__________
Date Purchased: __________
Tag Generation: __________

Value Totals: __________

40

Clubby II™

(exclusive to Beanie Babies® Official Club™ members)

Bear · N/A
Issued: March 31, 1999
Current - Hard To Find

Market Value:
[5]-$_____

Birthdate: March 9, 1999
Price Paid: $__________
Date Purchased: __________
Tag Generation: __________

A proud club member, named Clubby II
My color is special, a purplish hue
Take me along to your favorite place
Carry me in my platinum case!

41

Congo™

Gorilla · #4160
Issued: June 15, 1996
Retired: December 31, 1998

Market Value:
[5]-$12
[4]-$14

Birthdate: November 9, 1996
Price Paid: $__________
Date Purchased: __________
Tag Generation: __________

Black as the night and fierce is he
On the ground or in a tree
Strong and mighty as the Congo
He's related to our Bongo!

Value Totals: __________

42

Coral™

Fish · #4079
Issued: June 3, 1995
Retired: January 1, 1997

Market Value:
[4] - $175
[3] - $250

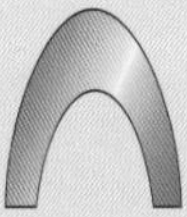

Coral is beautiful, as you know
Made of colors in the rainbow
Whether it's pink, yellow or blue
These colors were chosen just for you!

Birthdate: March 2, 1995
Price Paid: $__________
Date Purchased: __________
Tag Generation: __________

43

Crunch™

Shark · #4130
Issued: January 1, 1997
Retired: September 24, 1998

Market Value:
[5] - $12
[4] - $14

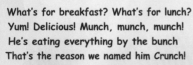

What's for breakfast? What's for lunch?
Yum! Delicious! Munch, munch, munch!
He's eating everything by the bunch
That's the reason we named him Crunch!

Birthdate: January 13, 1996
Price Paid: $__________
Date Purchased: __________
Tag Generation: __________

Value Totals: __________

Cubbie™

44

(name changed from "Brownie™")

ORIGINAL NINE

Bear · #4010
Issued: January 8, 1994
Retired: December 31, 1997

Market Value:
[5]-$32
[4]-$34
[3]-$175
[2]-$340
[1]-$530

Birthdate: November 14, 1993
Price Paid: $__________
Date Purchased: __________
Tag Generation: __________

Cubbie used to eat crackers and honey
And what happened to him was funny
He was stung by fourteen bees
Now Cubbie eats broccoli and cheese!

Curly™

45

Bear · #4052
Issued: June 15, 1996
Retired: December 31, 1998

Market Value:
[5]-$25
[4]-$30

Birthdate: April 12, 1996
Price Paid: $__________
Date Purchased: __________
Tag Generation: __________

A bear so cute with hair that's Curly
You will love and want him surely
To this bear always be true
He will be a friend to you!

46

Daisy™

Cow · #4006
Issued: June 25, 1994
Retired: September 15, 1998

Market Value:
[5]-$13
[4]-$16
[3]-$130
[2]-$250
[1]-$340

Daisy drinks milk each night
So her coat is shiny and bright
Milk is good for your hair and skin
What a way for your day to begin!

Birthdate: May 10, 1994
Price Paid: $__________
Date Purchased: __________
Tag Generation: __________

47

Derby™

Horse · #4008
Issued: June 3, 1995
Retired: May 26, 1999

Market Value:
A. Star/Fluffy Mane (Jan. 99 -May 99) [5]-$13
B. Star/Coarse Mane (Dec. 97-Dec. 98) [5]-$16
C. No Star/Coarse Mane (Est. Late 95–Dec. 97) [4]-$26 [3]-$450
D. No Star/Fine Mane (Est. June 95–Late 95) [3]-$3,100

B

C

D

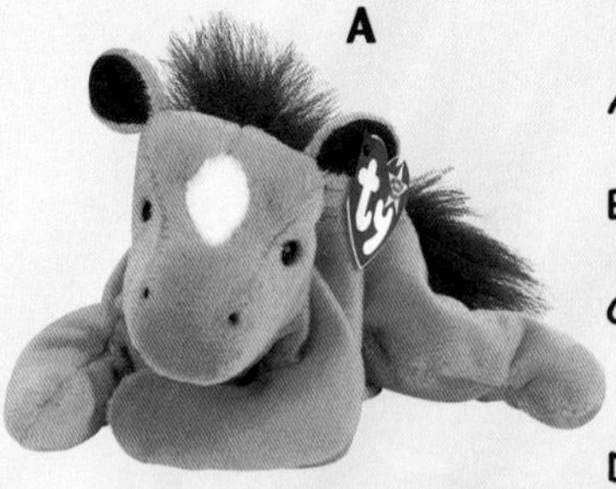
A

All the other horses used to tattle
Because Derby never wore his saddle
He left the stables, and the horses too
Just so Derby can be with you!

Birthdate: September 16, 1995
Price Paid: $__________
Date Purchased: __________
Tag Generation: __________

Value Totals: __________

Digger™

48

Crab · #4027
Issued: June 25, 1994
Retired: May 11, 1997

Market Value:
A. Red (June 95-May 97)
   ❹-$105
   ❸-$220
B. Orange (June 94–June 95)
   ❸-$650
   ❷-$700
   ❶-$835

B

A
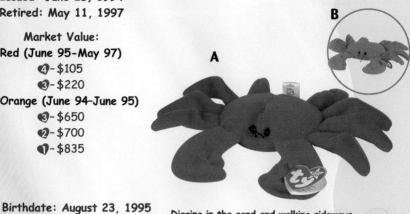

Birthdate: August 23, 1995
Price Paid: $_____
Date Purchased: _____
Tag Generation: _____

Digging in the sand and walking sideways
That's how Digger spends her days
Hard on the outside but sweet deep inside
Basking in the sun and riding the tide!

Doby™

49

Doberman · #4110
Issued: January 1, 1997
Retired: December 31, 1998

Market Value:
   ❺-$12
   ❹-$14

Birthdate: October 9, 1996
Price Paid: $_____
Date Purchased: _____
Tag Generation: _____

This dog is little but he has might
Keep him close when you sleep at night
He lays around with nothing to do
Until he sees it's time to protect you!

COLLECTOR'S
VALUE GUIDE™

Value
Totals: _____

50

Doodle™
(name changed to "Strut™")

Rooster · #4171
Issued: May 11, 1997
Retired: 1997

Market Value:
❹-$40

Listen closely to "cock-a-doodle-doo"
What's the rooster saying to you?
Hurry, wake up sleepy head
We have lots to do, get out of bed!

Birthdate: March 8, 1996
Price Paid: $_____
Date Purchased: _____
Tag Generation: _____

51

Dotty™

Dalmatian · #4100
Issued: May 11, 1997
Retired: December 31, 1998

Market Value:
❺-$13
❹-$15

The Beanies all thought it was a big joke
While writing her tag, their ink pen broke
She got in the way, and got all spotty
So now the Beanies call her Dotty!

Birthdate: October 17, 1996
Price Paid: $_____
Date Purchased: _____
Tag Generation: _____

Value
Totals: _____

COLLECTOR'S
VALUE GUIDE™

Early™

52

Robin · #4190
Issued: May 30, 1998
Current – Easy To Find

Market Value:
❺-$_____

Birthdate: March 20, 1997
Price Paid: $_____
Date Purchased: _____
Tag Generation: _____

Early is a red breasted robin
For a worm he'll soon be bobbin'
Always known as a sign of spring
This happy robin loves to sing!

Ears™

53

Rabbit · #4018
Issued: January 7, 1996
Retired: May 1, 1998

Market Value:
❺-$16
❹-$20
❸-$100

Birthdate: April 18, 1995
Price Paid: $_____
Date Purchased: _____
Tag Generation: _____

He's been eating carrots so long
Didn't understand what was wrong
Couldn't see the board during classes
Until the doctor gave him glasses!

Value
Totals: _____

54

Echo™

Dolphin · #4180
Issued: May 11, 1997
Retired: May 1, 1998

Market Value:
[5]-$18
[4]-$21

Echo the dolphin lives in the sea
Playing with her friends, like you and me
Through the waves she echoes the sound
"I'm so glad to have you around!"

Birthdate: December 21, 1996
Price Paid: $__________
Date Purchased: __________
Tag Generation: __________

55

Eggbert™

Chick · #4232
Issued: January 1, 1999
Retired: July 28, 1999

Market Value:
[5]-$14

Cracking her shell taking a peek
Look, she's playing hide and seek
Ready or not, here I come
Take me home and have some fun!

Birthdate: April 10, 1998
Price Paid: $__________
Date Purchased: __________
Tag Generation: __________

Value Totals: __________

56

Erin™

Bear · #4186
Issued: January 31, 1998
Retired: May 21, 1999

Market Value:
[5]-$25

Birthdate: March 17, 1997
Price Paid: $__________
Date Purchased: __________
Tag Generation: __________

Named after the beautiful Emerald Isle
This Beanie Baby will make you smile,
A bit of luck, a pot of gold,
Light up the faces, both young and old!

57

Eucalyptus™

Koala · #4240
Issued: April 8, 1999
Current - Moderate To Find

Market Value:
[5]-$_____

Birthdate: April 28, 1999
Price Paid: $__________
Date Purchased: __________
Tag Generation: __________

Koalas climb with grace and ease
To the top branches of the trees
Sleeping by day under a gentle breeze
Feeding at night on two pounds of leaves!

58

Ewey™

Lamb · #4219
Issued: January 1, 1999
Retired: July 19, 1999

Market Value:
[5]- $12

Needles and yarn, Ewey loves to knit
Making sweaters with perfect fit
Happy to make one for you and me
Showing off hers, for all to see!

Birthdate: March 1, 1998
Price Paid: $__________
Date Purchased: __________
Tag Generation: __________

59

Fetch™

Golden Retriever · #4189
Issued: May 30, 1998
Retired: December 31, 1998

Market Value:
[5]- $17

Fetch is alert at the crack of dawn
Walking through dew drops on the lawn
Always golden, loyal and true
This little puppy is the one for you!

Birthdate: February 4, 1997
Price Paid: $__________
Date Purchased: __________
Tag Generation: __________

Value Totals: __________

Flash™

60

Dolphin · #4021
Issued: January 8, 1994
Retired: May 11, 1997

Market Value:
❹-$115
❸-$180
❷-$350
❶-$475

Birthdate: May 13, 1993
Price Paid: $_____
Date Purchased: _____
Tag Generation: _____

You know dolphins are a smart breed
Our friend Flash knows how to read
Splash the whale is the one who taught her
Although reading is difficult under the water!

Fleece™

61

Lamb · #4125
Issued: January 1, 1997
Retired: December 31, 1998

Market Value:
❺-$12
❹-$14

Birthdate: March 21, 1996
Price Paid: $_____
Date Purchased: _____
Tag Generation: _____

Fleece would like to sing a lullaby
But please be patient, she's rather shy
When you sleep, keep her by your ear
Her song will leave you nothing to fear.

62

Flip™

Cat · #4012
Issued: January 7, 1996
Retired: October 1, 1997

Market Value:
❹-$38
❸-$115

Flip the cat is an acrobat
She loves playing on her mat
This cat flips with such grace and flair
She can somersault in mid air!

Birthdate: February 28, 1995
Price Paid: $_____
Date Purchased: _____
Tag Generation: _____

63

NEW!

Flitter™

Butterfly · #4255
Issued: Summer 1999
Current – Very Hard To Find

Market Value:
❺-$_____

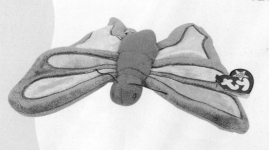

I did not know what I was to be
Covered in fuzz, it was hard to see
Now a butterfly, what a beautiful sight
On silken wings I take to flight!

Birthdate: June 2, 1999
Price Paid: $_____
Date Purchased: _____
Tag Generation: _____

Value
Totals: _____

COLLECTOR'S
VALUE GUIDE™

Floppity™

64

Bunny · #4118
Issued: January 1, 1997
Retired: May 1, 1998

Market Value:
⑤- $20
④- $23

Birthdate: May 28, 1996
Price Paid: $_____
Date Purchased: _____
Tag Generation: _____

Floppity hops from here to there
Searching for eggs without a care
Lavender coat from head to toe
All dressed up and nowhere to go!

Flutter™

65

Butterfly · #4043
Issued: June 3, 1995
Retired: June 15, 1996

Market Value:
③- $925

Birthdate: N/A
Price Paid: $_____
Date Purchased: _____
Tag Generation: _____

No Poem_____
_____
_____
_____

COLLECTOR'S
VALUE GUIDE™

Value
Totals: _____

66

Fortune™

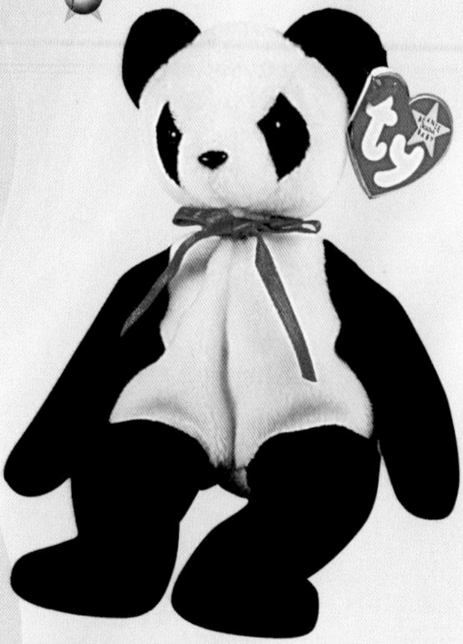

Panda · #4196
Issued: May 30, 1998
Retired: August 24, 1999

Market Value:
[5]- $_____

Nibbling on a bamboo tree
This little panda is hard to see
You're so lucky with this one you found
Only a few are still around!

Birthdate: December 6, 1997
Price Paid: $__________
Date Purchased: __________
Tag Generation: __________

67

Freckles™

Leopard · #4066
Issued: June 15, 1996
Retired: December 31, 1998

Market Value:
[5]- $13
[4]- $15

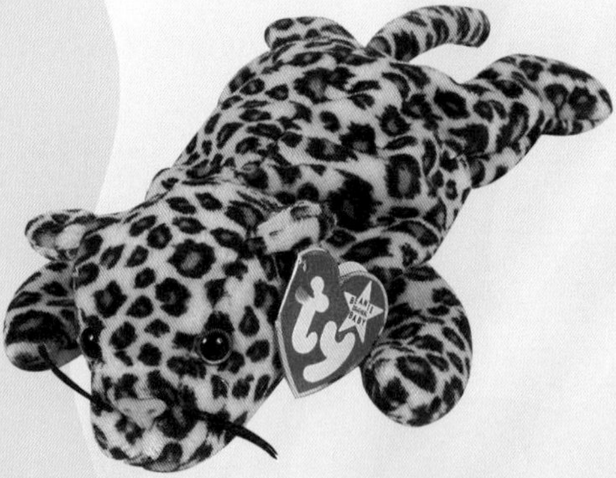

From the trees he hunts prey
In the night and in the day
He's the king of camouflage
Look real close, he's no mirage!

Birthdate: June 3, 1996
or July 28, 1996
Price Paid: $__________
Date Purchased: __________
Tag Generation: __________

Value Totals: __________

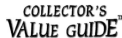

Fuzz™

Bear · #4237
Issued: January 1, 1999
Current – Hard To Find

Market Value:
❺-$_____

Birthdate: July 23, 1998
Price Paid: $_____
Date Purchased: _____
Tag Generation: _____

Look closely at this handsome bear
His texture is really quite rare.
With golden highlights in his hair
He has class, style and flair!

Garcia™

Bear · #4051
Issued: January 7, 1996
Retired: May 11, 1997

Market Value:
❹-$190
❸-$260

Birthdate: August 1, 1995
Price Paid: $_____
Date Purchased: _____
Tag Generation: _____

The Beanies use to follow him around
Because Garcia traveled from town to town
He's pretty popular as you can see
Some even say he's legendary!

Value
Totals: _____

70

Germania™
(exclusive to Germany)

Bear · #4236
Issued: January 1, 1999
Current – Impossible To Find

Market Value
(in U.S. market):
❺-$300

> POEM TRANSLATION
> Unity and Justice and Freedom
> Is the song of German unity.
> All good little girls and boys
> Should love this little German bear.

Einigkeit und Recht und Freiheit
ist der Deutschen Einheistlied.
Allen Kindern brav und fein
soll dieser Bär das Liebste sein.

Geburtstag: Oktober 3, 1990
Price Paid: $_____
Date Purchased: _____
Tag Generation: _____

71

GiGi™

Poodle · #4191
Issued: May 30, 1998
Current – Easy To Find

Market Value:
❺-$_____

Prancing and dancing all down the street
Thinking her hairdo is oh so neat
Always so careful in the wind and rain
She's a dog that is anything but plain!

Birthdate: April 7, 1997
Price Paid: $_____
Date Purchased: _____
Tag Generation: _____

Value
Totals: _____

COLLECTOR'S
VALUE GUIDE™

72

Glory™

Bear • #4188
Issued: May 30, 1998
Retired: December 31, 1998

Market Value:
[5]-$40

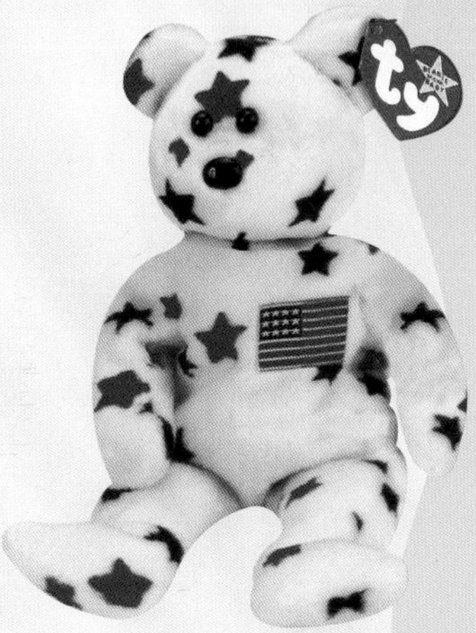

Birthdate: July 4, 1997
Price Paid: $__________
Date Purchased: __________
Tag Generation: __________

Wearing the flag for all to see
Symbol of freedom for you and me
Red white and blue - Independence Day
Happy Birthday USA!

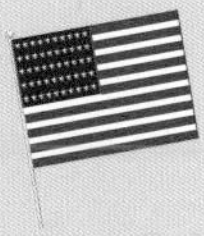

73

Goatee™

Mountain Goat • #4235
Issued: January 1, 1999
Current - Easy To Find

Market Value:
[5]-$_____

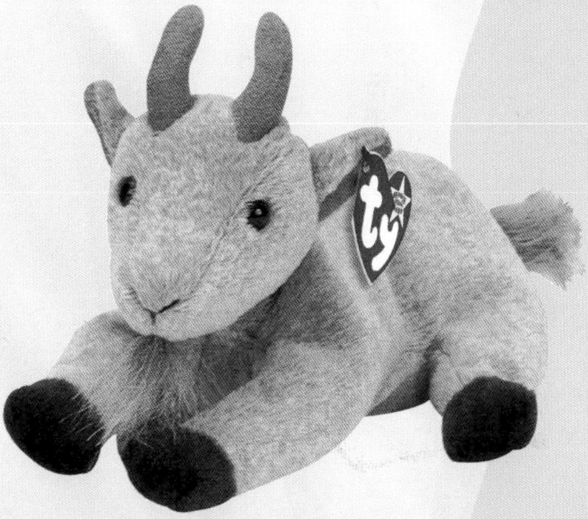

Birthdate: November 4, 1998
Price Paid: $__________
Date Purchased: __________
Tag Generation: __________

Though she's hungry, she's in a good mood
Searching through garbage, tin cans for food
For Goatee the goat, it's not a big deal
Anything at all makes a fine meal!

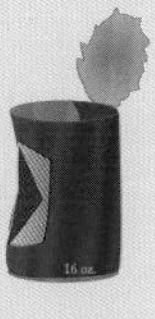

Value Totals: __________

74

Gobbles™

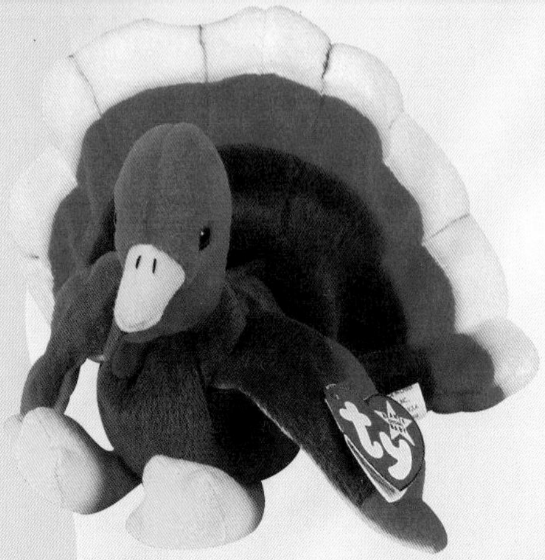

Turkey · #4034
Issued: October 1, 1997
Retired: March 31, 1999

Market Value:
[5] - $12
[4] - $14

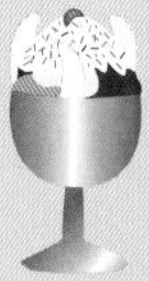

Gobbles the turkey loves to eat
Once a year she has a feast
I have a secret I'd like to divulge
If she eats too much her tummy will bulge!

Birthdate: November 27, 1996
Price Paid: $__________
Date Purchased: __________
Tag Generation: __________

75

Goldie™

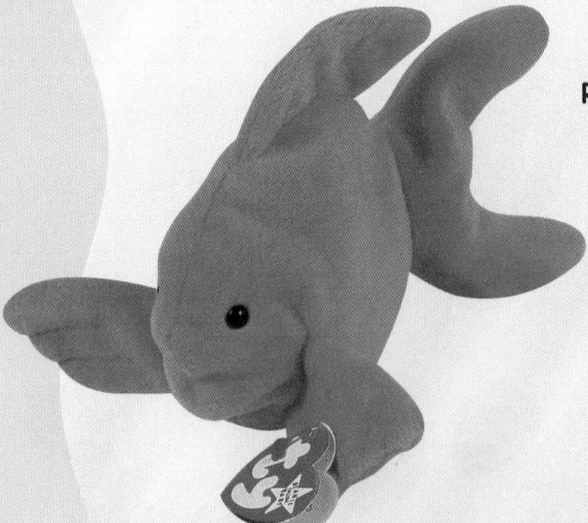

Goldfish · #4023
Issued: June 25, 1994
Retired: December 31, 1997

Market Value:
[5] - $45
[4] - $45
[3] - $115
[2] - $250
[1] - $415

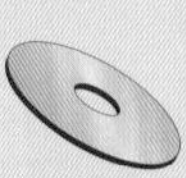

She's got rhythm, she's got soul
What more to like in a fish bowl?
Through sound waves Goldie swam
Because this goldfish likes to jam!

Birthdate: November 14, 1994
Price Paid: $__________
Date Purchased: __________
Tag Generation: __________

Value Totals: __________

Goochy™

Jellyfish · #4230
Issued: January 1, 1999
Current – Easy To Find

Market Value:
➎-$_____

Birthdate: November 18, 1998
Price Paid: $_____
Date Purchased: _____
Tag Generation: _____

Swirl, swish, squirm and wiggle
Listen closely, hear him giggle
The most ticklish jellyfish you'll ever meet
Even though he has no feet!

Gracie™

Swan · #4126
Issued: January 1, 1997
Retired: May 1, 1998

Market Value:
➎-$17
➍-$19

Birthdate: June 17, 1996
Price Paid: $_____
Date Purchased: _____
Tag Generation: _____

As a duckling, she was confused,
Birds on the lake were quite amused.
Poking fun until she would cry,
Now the most beautiful swan at Ty!

COLLECTOR'S
VALUE GUIDE™

Value
Totals: _____

78

NEW!

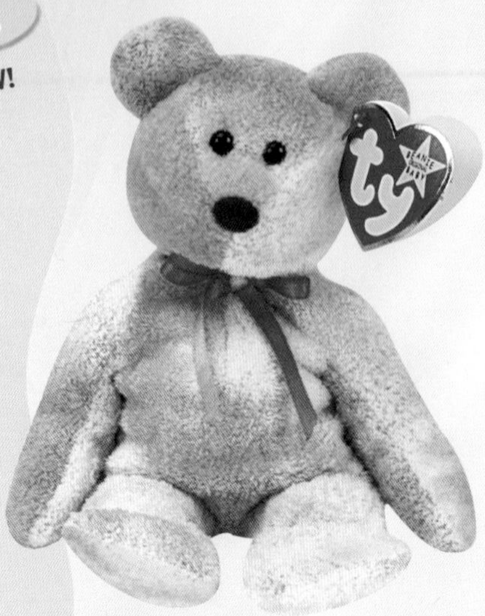

Groovy™

Bear · #4256
Issued: August 31, 1999
Current – Just Released

Market Value:
[5]-$_____

Wearing colors of the rainbow
Making good friends wherever I go
Take me with you, don't let me stay
I need your love all night and day!

Birthdate: January 10, 1999
Price Paid: $__________
Date Purchased: __________
Tag Generation: __________

79

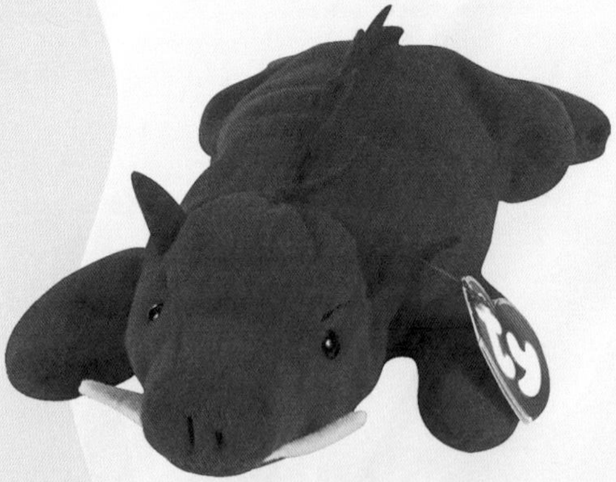

Grunt™

Razorback · #4092
Issued: January 7, 1996
Retired: May 11, 1997

Market Value:
[4]-$150
[3]-$215

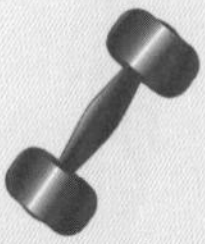

Some Beanies think Grunt is tough
No surprise, he's scary enough
But if you take him home you'll see
Grunt is the sweetest Beanie Baby!

Birthdate: July 19, 1995
Price Paid: $__________
Date Purchased: __________
Tag Generation: __________

Value Totals: __________

80

Halo™

Angel Bear · #4208
Issued: September 30, 1998
Current – Moderate To Find

Market Value:
[5]-$_____

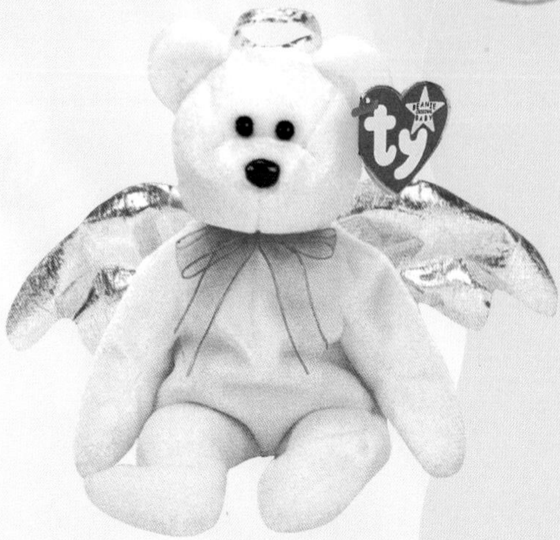

Birthdate: August 31, 1998
Price Paid: $__________
Date Purchased: __________
Tag Generation: __________

When you sleep, I'm always here
Don't be afraid, I am near
Watching over you with lots of love
Your guardian angel from up above!

81

Happy™

Hippo · #4061
Issued: June 25, 1994
Retired: May 1, 1998

Market Value:
A. Lavender (June 95–May 98)
[5]-$26
[4]-$28
[3]-$210
B. Gray (June 94–June 95)
[3]-$625
[2]-$700
[1]-$775

A
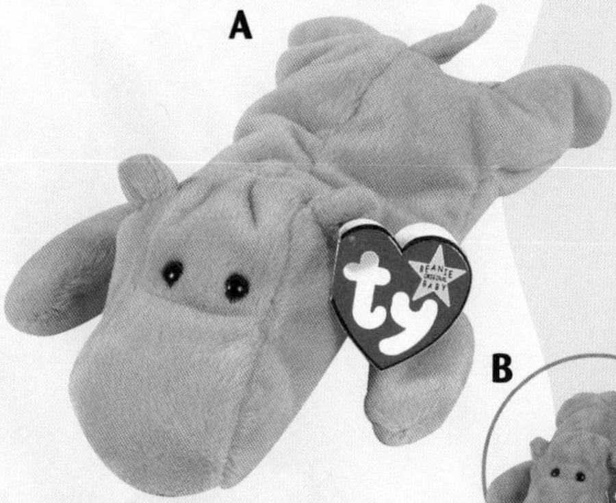

B
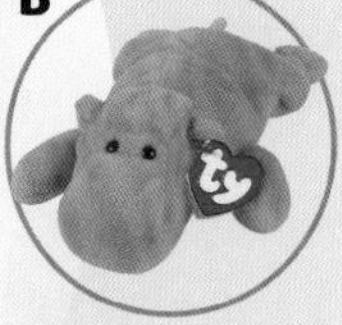

Birthdate: February 25, 1994
Price Paid: $__________
Date Purchased: __________
Tag Generation: __________

Happy the Hippo loves to wade
In the river and in the shade
When Happy shoots water out of his snout
You know he's happy without a doubt!

Value Totals: __________

82

Hippie™

Bunny · #4218
Issued: January 1, 1999
Retired: July 12, 1999

Market Value:
[5]-$23

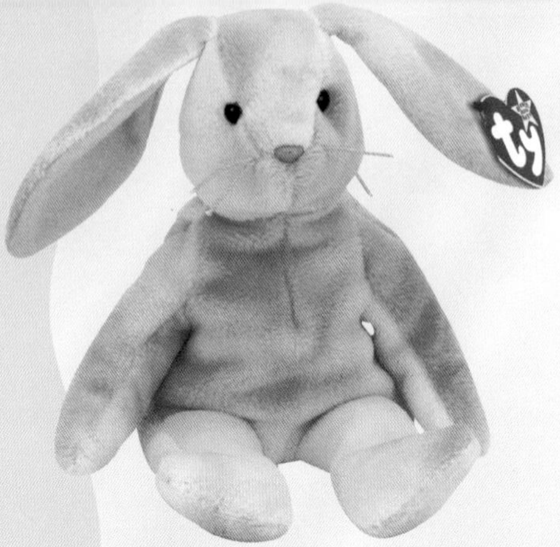

Hippie fell into the dye, they say
While coloring eggs, one spring day
From the tips of his ears, down to his toes
Colors of springtime, he proudly shows!

Birthdate: May 4, 1998
Price Paid: $__________
Date Purchased: __________
Tag Generation: __________

83

Hippity™

Bunny · #4119
Issued: January 1, 1997
Retired: May 1, 1998

Market Value:
[5]-$23
[4]-$26

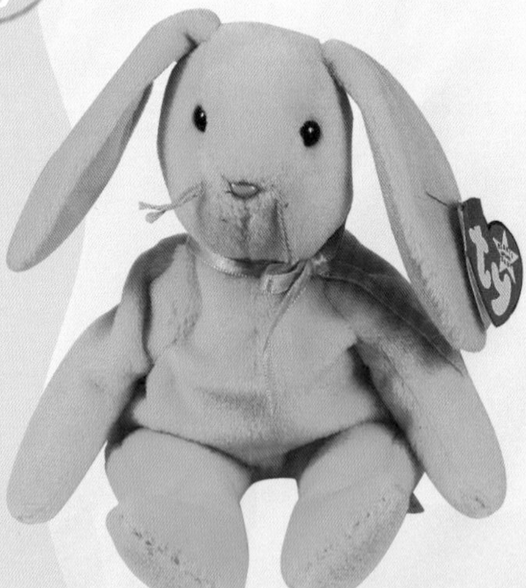

Hippity is a cute little bunny
Dressed in green, he looks quite funny
Twitching his nose in the air
Sniffing a flower here and there!

Birthdate: June 1, 1996
Price Paid: $__________
Date Purchased: __________
Tag Generation: __________

Value Totals: __________

84

Hissy™

Snake · #4185
Issued: December 31, 1997
Retired: March 31, 1999

Market Value:
[5]- $11

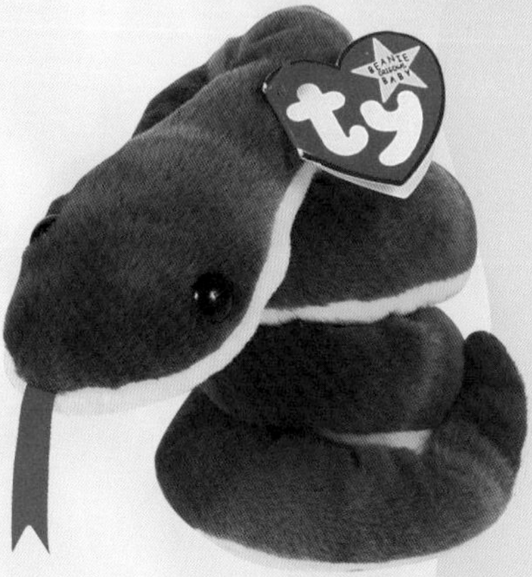

Birthdate: April 4, 1997
Price Paid: $__________
Date Purchased: __________
Tag Generation: __________

Curled and coiled and ready to play
He waits for you patiently every day
He'll keep his best friend, but not his skin
And stay with you through thick and thin.

85

NEW!

Honks™

Goose · #4258
Issued: August 31, 1999
Current - Just Released

Market Value:
[5]- $_____

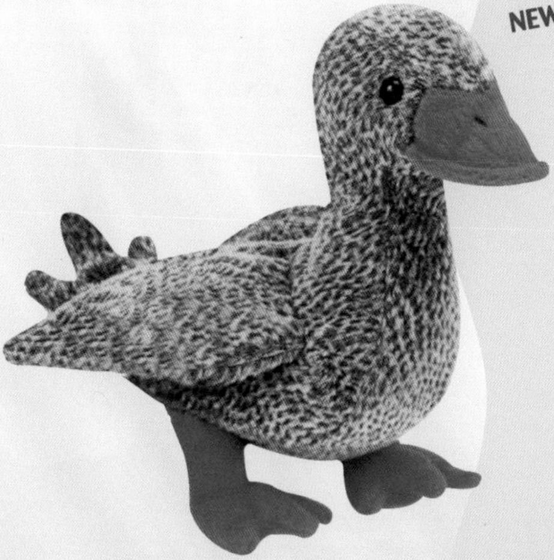

Birthdate: March 11, 1999
Price Paid: $__________
Date Purchased: __________
Tag Generation: __________

Honks the goose likes to fly away
South for Winter he will stay
When Spring comes back, North he will fly
And swim in ponds and lakes nearby!

Value Totals: __________

86

Hoot™

Owl · #4073
Issued: January 7, 1996
Retired: October 1, 1997

Market Value:
❹ – $45
❸ – $110

Late to bed, late to rise
Nevertheless, Hoot's quite wise
Studies by candlelight, nothing new
Like a president, do you know Whooo?

Birthdate: August 9, 1995
Price Paid: $_____
Date Purchased: _____
Tag Generation: _____

87

Hope™

Bear · #4213
Issued: January 1, 1999
Current - Moderate To Find

Market Value:
❺ – $_____

Every night when it's time for bed
Fold your hands and bow your head
An angelic face, a heart that's true
You have a friend to pray with you!

Birthdate: March 23, 1998
Price Paid: $_____
Date Purchased: _____
Tag Generation: _____

Value
Totals: _____

COLLECTOR'S
VALUE GUIDE™

88

Hoppity™

Bunny · #4117
Issued: January 1, 1997
Retired: May 1, 1998

Market Value:
[5]-$20
[4]-$23

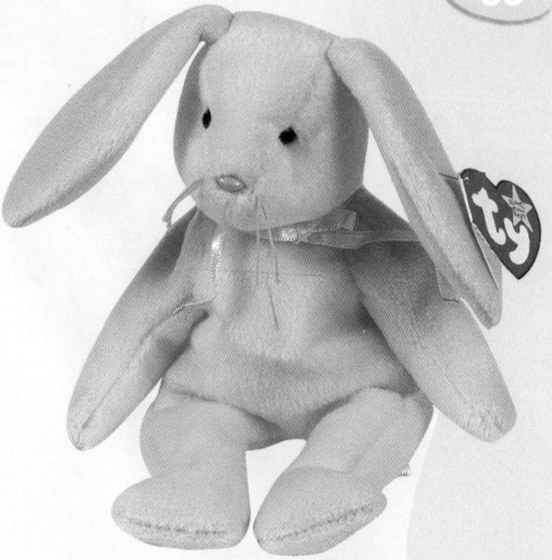

Birthdate: April 3, 1996
Price Paid: $__________
Date Purchased: __________
Tag Generation: __________

Hopscotch is what she likes to play
If you don't join in, she'll hop away
So play a game if you have the time,
She likes to play, rain or shine!

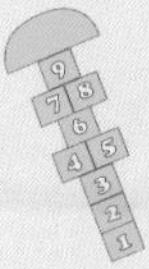

89

Humphrey™

Camel · #4060
Issued: June 25, 1994
Retired: June 15, 1995

Market Value:
[3]-$2,100
[2]-$2,200
[1]-$2,400

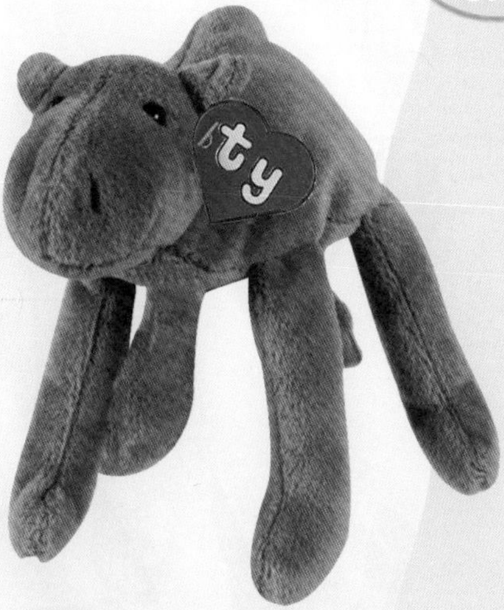

Birthdate: N/A
Price Paid: $__________
Date Purchased: __________
Tag Generation: __________

No Poem

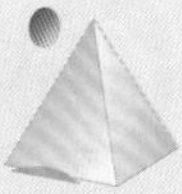

Value Totals: __________

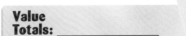

90

Iggy™

Iguana · #4038
Issued: December 31, 1997
Retired: March 31, 1999

B
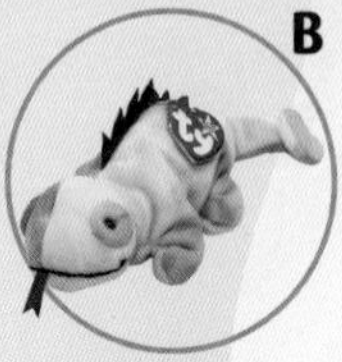

A
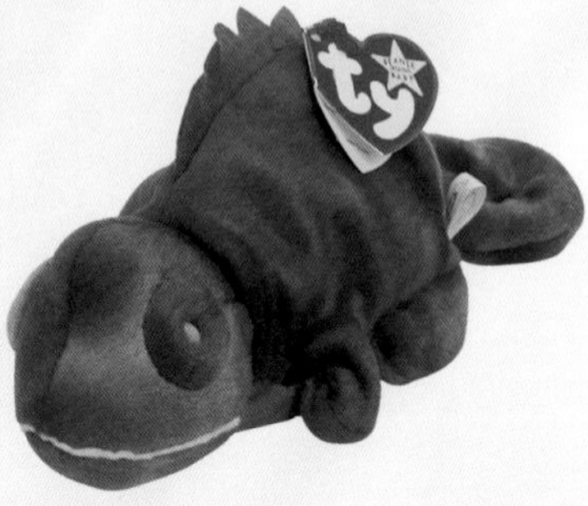

C
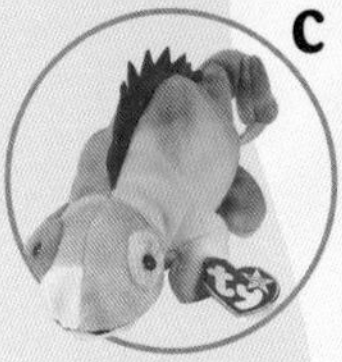

Market Value:

A. Blue/No Tongue (Mid 98–March 99)
[5] - $13

B. Tie-dye/With Tongue (June 98–Mid 98)
[5] - $13

C. Tie-dye/No Tongue (Dec. 97–June 98)
[5] - $13

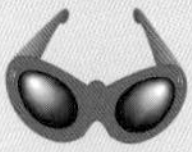

Sitting on a rock, basking in the sun
Is this iguana's idea of fun
Towel and glasses, book and beach chair
His life is so perfect without a care!

Birthdate: August 12, 1997
Price Paid: $__________
Date Purchased: __________
Tag Generation: __________

91

Inch™

Inchworm · #4044
Issued: June 3, 1995
Retired: May 1, 1998

B
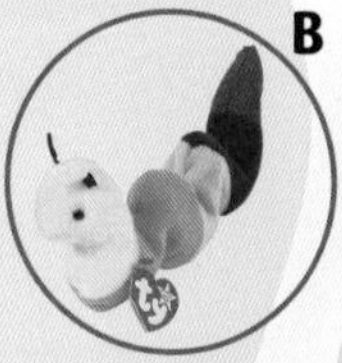

A
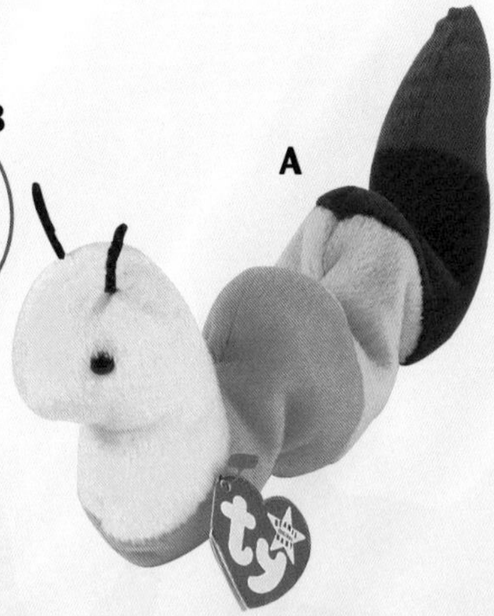

Market Value:

A. Yarn Antennas (Oct. 97–May 98)
[5] - $25
[4] - $28

B. Felt Antennas (June 95–Oct. 97)
[4] - $160
[3] - $190

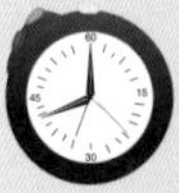

Inch the worm is a friend of mine
He goes so slow all the time
Inching around from here to there
Traveling the world without a care!

Birthdate: September 3, 1995
Price Paid: $__________
Date Purchased: __________
Tag Generation: __________

Value Totals: __________

92

Inky™

Octopus · #4028
Issued: June 25, 1994
Retired: May 1, 1998

Market Value:
A. Pink (June 95-May 98)
[5]-$30 [4]-$33
[3]-$205
B. Tan With Mouth
(Sept. 94-June 95)
[3]-$625 [2]-$700
C. Tan Without Mouth
(June 94-Sept. 94)
[2]-$775 [1]-$870

A

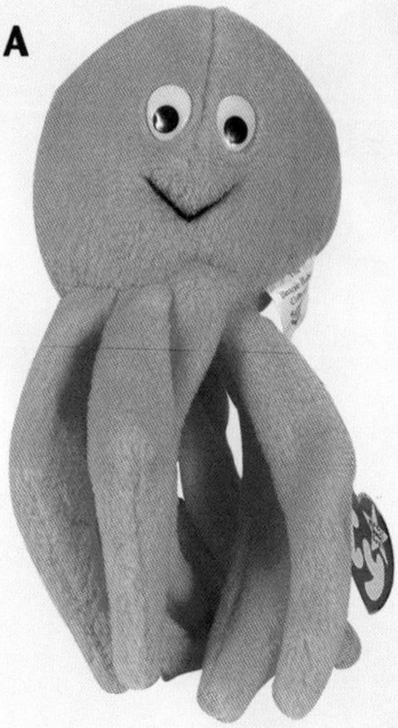

B

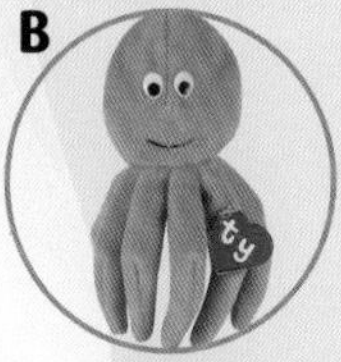

C

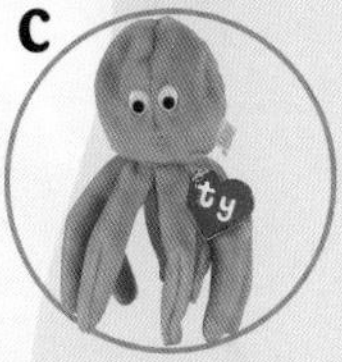

Birthdate: November 29, 1994
Price Paid: $__________
Date Purchased: __________
Tag Generation: __________

Inky's head is big and round
As he swims he makes no sound
If you need a hand, don't hesitate
Inky can help because he has eight!

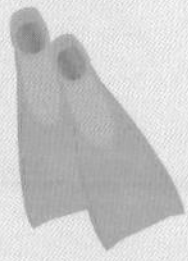

93

Jabber™

Parrot · #4197
Issued: May 30, 1998
Current - Easy To Find

Market Value:
[5]-$_____

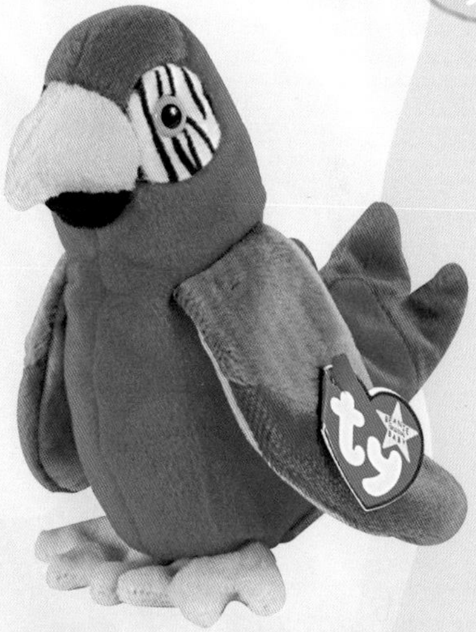

Birthdate: October 10, 1997
Price Paid: $__________
Date Purchased: __________
Tag Generation: __________

Teaching Jabber to move his beak
A large vocabulary he now can speak
Jabber will repeat what you say
Teach him a new word everyday!

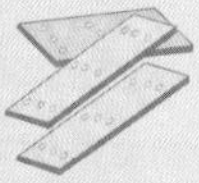

Value Totals: __________

94

Jake™

Mallard Duck • #4199
Issued: May 30, 1998
Current – Easy To Find

Market Value:
❤5– $_____

Jake the drake likes to splash in a puddle
Take him home and give him a cuddle
Quack, Quack, Quack, he will say
He's so glad you're here to play!

Birthdate: April 16, 1997
Price Paid: $_____
Date Purchased: _____
Tag Generation: _____

95

Jolly™

Walrus • #4082
Issued: May 11, 1997
Retired: May 1, 1998

Market Value:
❤5– $16
❤4– $18

Jolly the walrus is not very serious
He laughs and laughs until he's delirious
He often reminds me of my dad
Always happy, never sad!

Birthdate: December 2, 1996
Price Paid: $_____
Date Purchased: _____
Tag Generation: _____

Value Totals: _____

COLLECTOR'S
VALUE GUIDE™

96

Kicks™

Bear · #4229
Issued: January 1, 1999
Current - Moderate To Find

Market Value:
[5]- $_____

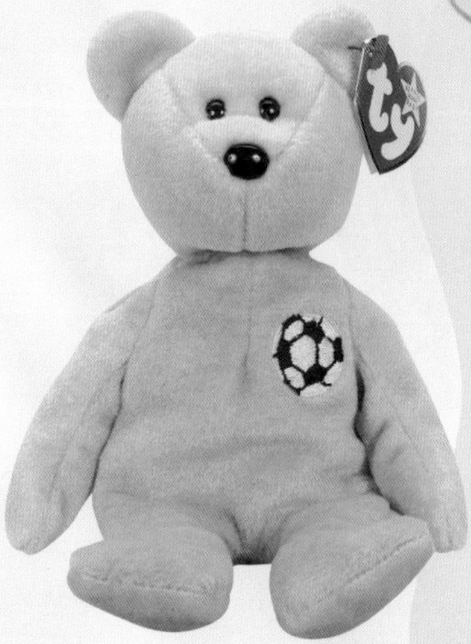

Birthdate: August 16, 1998
Price Paid: $__________
Date Purchased: __________
Tag Generation: __________

The world cup is his dream
Kicks the bear is the best on his team
He hopes that one day he'll be the pick
First he needs to improve his kick!

97

Kiwi™

Toucan · #4070
Issued: June 3, 1995
Retired: January 1, 1997

Market Value:
[4]- $165
[3]- $230

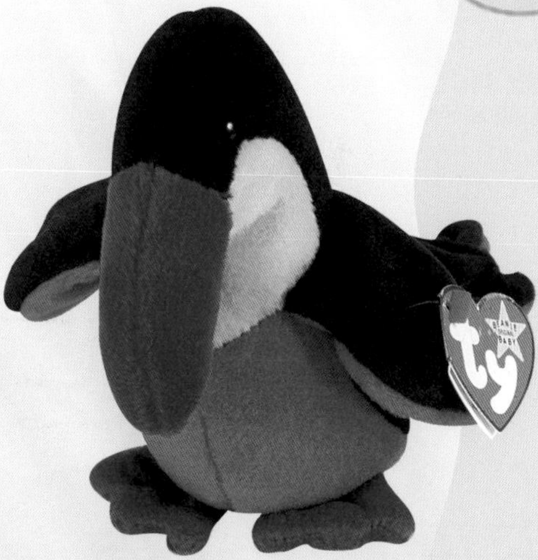

Birthdate: September 16, 1995
Price Paid: $__________
Date Purchased: __________
Tag Generation: __________

Kiwi waits for the April showers
Watching a garden bloom with flowers
There trees grow with fruit that's sweet
I'm sure you'll guess his favorite treat!

98

Knuckles™

Pig · #4247
Issued: April 14, 1999
Current – Moderate To Find

Market Value:
[5]-$_____

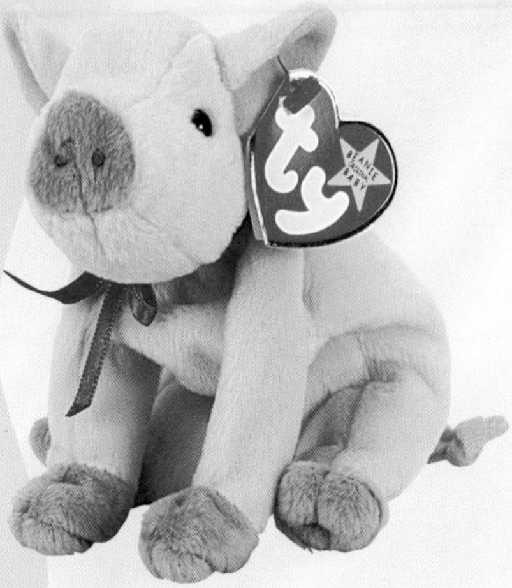

In the kitchen working hard
Using ingredients from the yard
No one will eat it, can you guess why?
Her favorite recipe is for mud pie!

Birthdate: March 25, 1999
Price Paid: $__________
Date Purchased: __________
Tag Generation: __________

99

KuKu™

Cockatoo · #4192
Issued: May 30, 1998
Current – Easy To Find

Market Value:
[5]-$_____

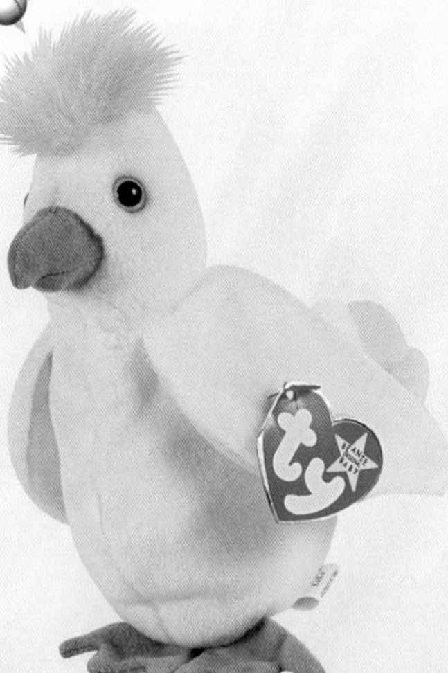

This fancy bird loves to converse
He talks in poems, rhythms and verse
So take him home and give him some time
You'll be surprised how he can rhyme!

Birthdate: January 5, 1997
Price Paid: $__________
Date Purchased: __________
Tag Generation: __________

Value Totals: __________

Lefty™

Donkey · #4085
Issued: June 15, 1996
Retired: January 1, 1997

Market Value:
❹-$250

Birthdate: July 4, 1996
Price Paid: $_____
Date Purchased: _____
Tag Generation: _____

Donkeys to the left, elephants to the right
Often seems like a crazy sight
This whole game seems very funny
Until you realize they're spending
Your money!

Legs™

Frog · #4020
Issued: January 8, 1994
Retired: October 1, 1997

Market Value:
❹-$23
❸-$100
❷-$340
❶-$440

Birthdate: April 25, 1993
Price Paid: $_____
Date Purchased: _____
Tag Generation: _____

Legs lives in a hollow log
Legs likes to play leap frog
If you like to hang out at the lake
Legs will be the new friend you'll make!

Value
Totals: _____

102

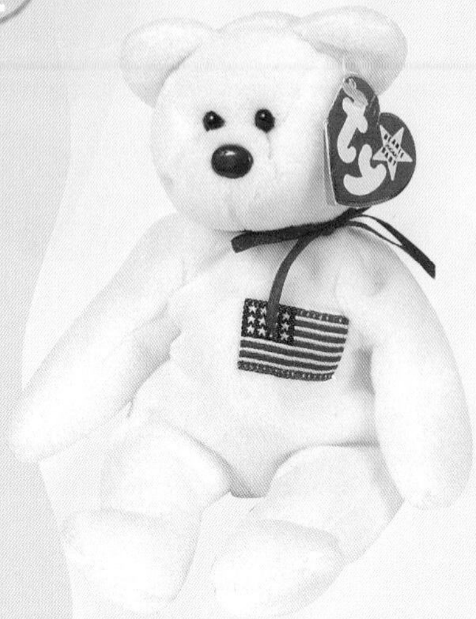

Libearty™

Bear · #4057
Issued: June 15, 1996
Retired: January 1, 1997

Market Value:
[4]-$360

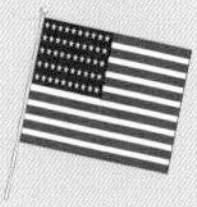

I am called libearty
I wear the flag for all to see
Hope and freedom is my way
That's why I wear flag USA

Birthdate: Summer 1996
Price Paid: $__________
Date Purchased: __________
Tag Generation: __________

103

NEW!

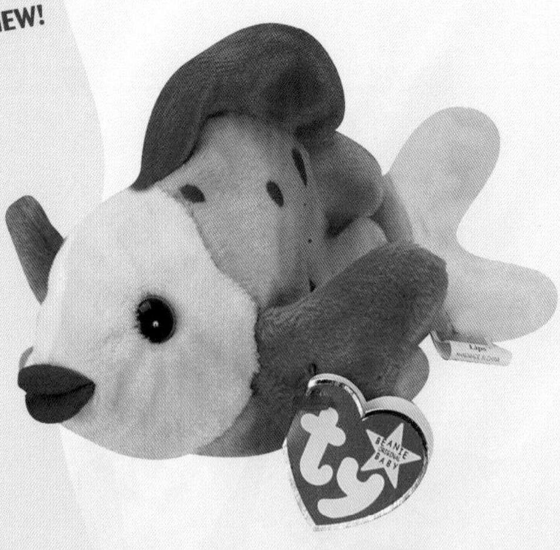

Lips™

Fish · #4254
Issued: Summer 1999
Current - Very Hard To Find

Market Value:
[5]-$_____

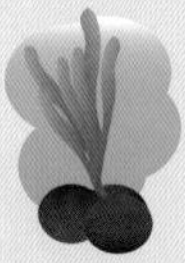

Did you ever see a fish like me?
I'm the most colorful in the sea
Traveling with friends in a school
Swimming all day is really cool!

Birthdate: March 15, 1999
Price Paid: $__________
Date Purchased: __________
Tag Generation: __________

Value Totals: __________

104

Lizzy™

Lizard · #4033
Issued: June 3, 1995
Retired: December 31, 1997

Market Value:
A. Blue (Jan. 96-Dec. 97)
[5]-$26
[4]-$28
[3]-$250
B. Tie-dye (June 95–Jan. 96)
[3]-$875

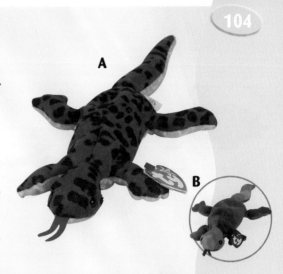

A

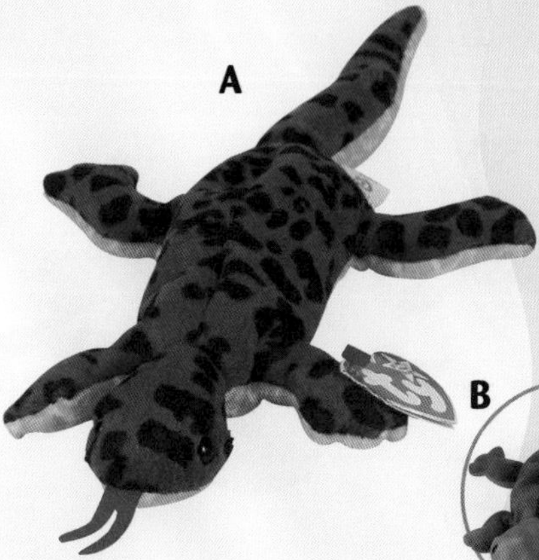

B

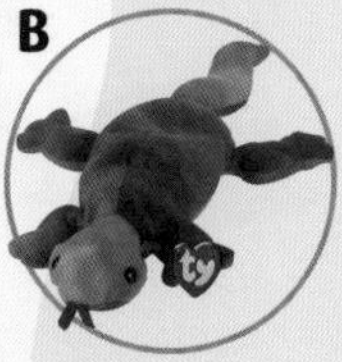

Birthdate: May 11, 1995
Price Paid: $__________
Date Purchased: __________
Tag Generation: __________

Lizzy loves Legs the frog
She hides with him under logs
Both of them search for flies
Underneath the clear blue skies!

105

Loosy™

Goose · #4206
Issued: September 30, 1998
Retired: September 1, 1999

Market Value:
[5]-$13

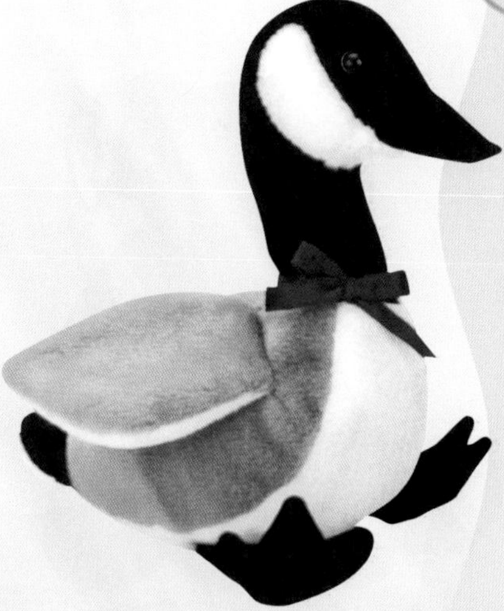

Birthdate: March 29, 1998
Price Paid: $__________
Date Purchased: __________
Tag Generation: __________

A tale has been told
Of a goose that laid gold
But try as she might
Loosy's eggs are just white!

Value Totals: __________

106

Lucky™

Ladybug · #4040
Issued: June 25, 1994
Retired: May 1, 1998

Market Value:
A. Approx. 11 Printed Spots
   (Feb. 96-May 98)
   5- $25 **4**- $25
B. Approx. 21 Printed Spots
   (Est. Mid 96-Late 96)
   4- $430
C. Approx. 7 Felt Glued-On
   Spots (June 94-Feb. 96)
   3- $210 **2**- $380
   1- $575

B   **A**

C

Lucky the lady bug loves the lotto
"Someone must win" that's her motto
But save your dimes and even a penny
Don't spend on the lotto and
You'll have many!

Birthdate: May 1, 1995
Price Paid: $_____
Date Purchased: _____
Tag Generation: _____

107

Luke™

Black Lab · #4214
Issued: January 1, 1999
Current – Easy To Find

Market Value:
5- $_____

After chewing on your favorite shoes
Luke gets tired, takes a snooze
Who wouldn't love a puppy like this?
Give him a hug, he'll give you a kiss!

Birthdate: June 15, 1998
Price Paid: $_____
Date Purchased: _____
Tag Generation: _____

Value
Totals: _____

COLLECTOR'S
VALUE GUIDE™

108

Mac™

Cardinal · #4225
Issued: January 1, 1999
Current – Easy To Find

Market Value:
[5]- $_____

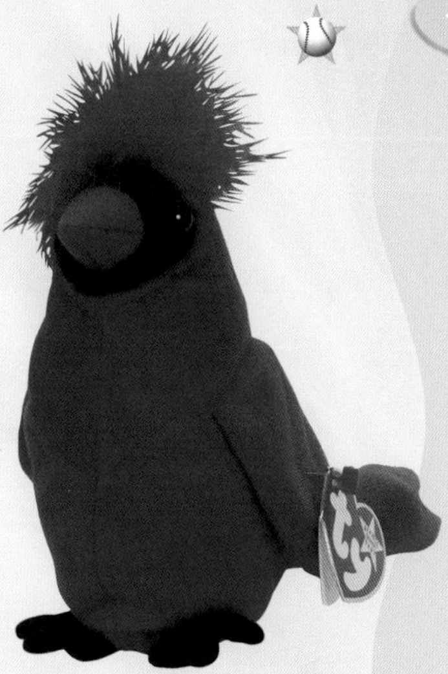

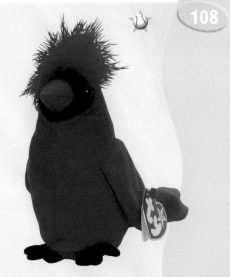

Birthdate: June 10, 1998
Price Paid: $__________
Date Purchased: __________
Tag Generation: __________

Mac tries hard to prove he's the best
Swinging his bat harder than the rest
Breaking records, enjoying the game
Hitting home runs is his claim to fame!

109

Magic™

Dragon · #4088
Issued: June 3, 1995
Retired: December 31, 1997

Market Value:
A. Pale Pink Thread
(June 95-Dec. 97)
[4]- $50
[3]- $145
B. Hot Pink Thread
(Est. Mid 96-Early 97)
[4]- $65

A

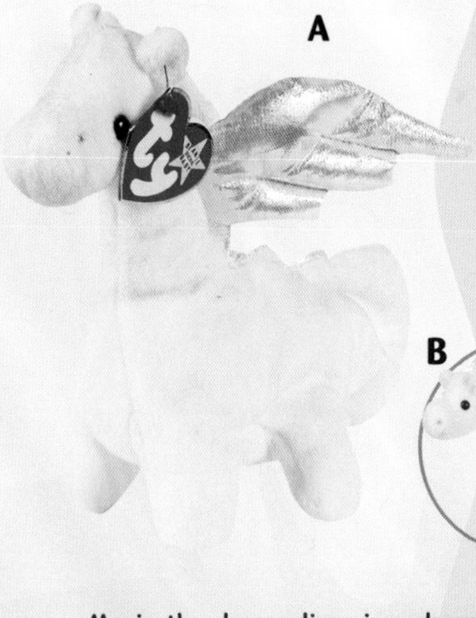

B

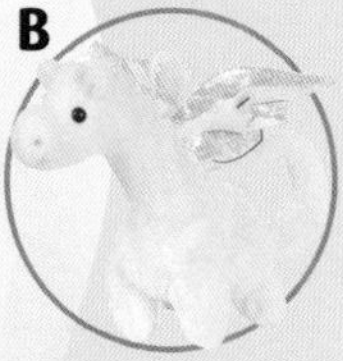

Birthdate: September 5, 1995
Price Paid: $__________
Date Purchased: __________
Tag Generation: __________

Magic the dragon lives in a dream
The most beautiful that you have ever seen
Through magic lands she likes to fly
Look up and watch her, way up high!

Value Totals: __________

110

Manny™

Manatee · #4081
Issued: January 7, 1996
Retired: May 11, 1997

Market Value:
❹- $150
❸- $230

Manny is sometimes called a sea cow
She likes to twirl and likes to bow
Manny sure is glad you bought her
Because it's so lonely under water!

Birthdate: June 8, 1995
Price Paid: $_____
Date Purchased: _____
Tag Generation: _____

111

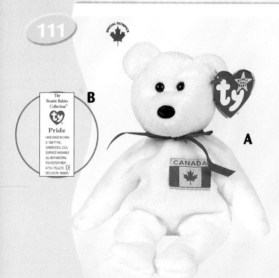

Maple™
(exclusive to Canada)

Bear · #4600
Issued: January 1, 1997
Current – Impossible To Find

Market Value
(in U.S. market):
A. "Maple™" Tush Tag
(Est. Early 97-Current)
❺- $180
❹- $215
B. "Pride™" Tush Tag
(Est. Early 97)
❹- $600

Birthdate: July 1, 1996
Price Paid: $_____
Date Purchased: _____
Tag Generation: _____

The
Beanie Babies
Collection™
Pride
HAND MADE IN CHINA
© 1997 TY INC.
OAKBROOK IL, USA
SURFACE WASHABLE
ALL NEW MATERIAL
POLYESTER FIBER
& PVC PELLETS CE
REG. NO. PA. 1965895

B

A

Maple the bear likes to ski
With his friends, he plays hockey.
He loves his pancakes and eats every crumb
Can you guess which country he's from?

Value
Totals: _____

COLLECTOR'S
VALUE GUIDE™

Mel™

112

Koala • #4162
Issued: January 1, 1997
Retired: March 31, 1999

Market Value:
[5] - $11
[4] - $13

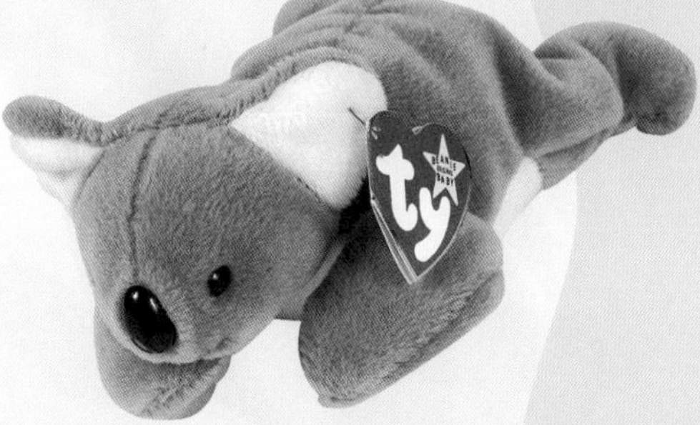

Birthdate: January 15, 1996
Price Paid: $__________
Date Purchased: __________
Tag Generation: __________

How do you name a Koala bear?
It's rather tough, I do declare!
It confuses me, I get into a funk
I'll name him Mel, after my favorite hunk!

Millennium™

113

Bear • #4226
Issued: January 1, 1999
Current - Hard To Find

Market Value:

A. "Millennium™" On Both Tags (Early 99-Current)
[5] - $_____

B. "Millenium™" Swing Tag & "Millennium™" Tush Tag (Early 99)
[5] - $30

C. "Millenium™" On Both Tags (Jan. 99-Early 99)
[5] - $30

A

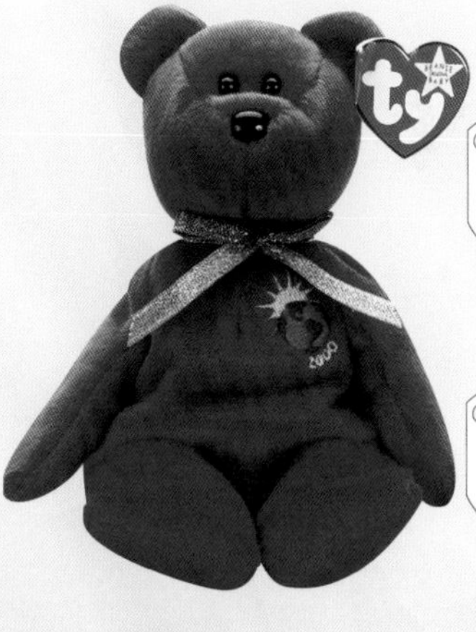

B

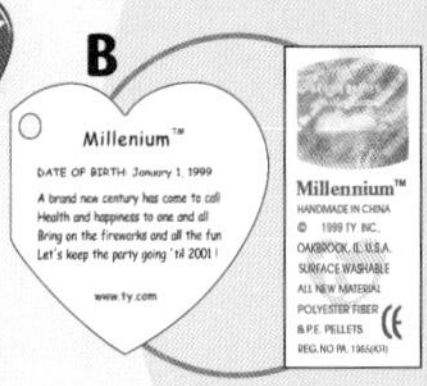

C

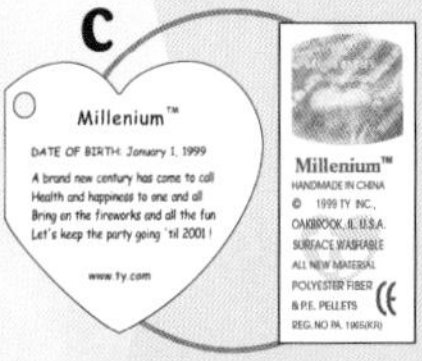

Birthdate: January 1, 1999
Price Paid: $__________
Date Purchased: __________
Tag Generation: __________

A brand new century has come to call
Health and happiness to one and all
Bring on the fireworks and all the fun
Let's keep the party going 'til 2001!

114

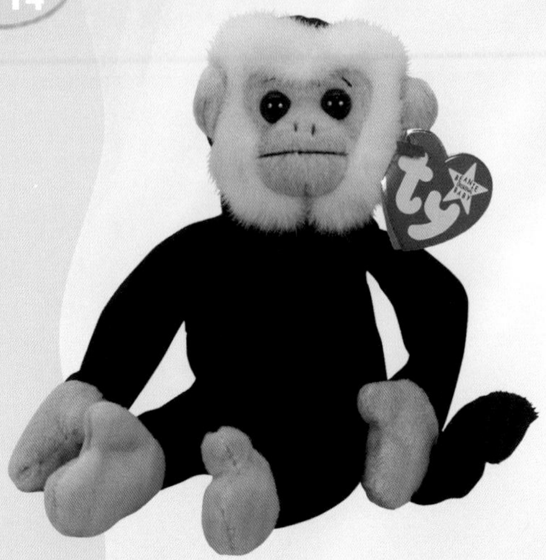

Mooch™

Spider Monkey · #4224
Issued: January 1, 1999
Current - Easy To Find

Market Value:
[5]-$_____

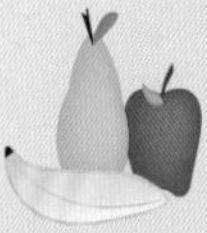

Look in the treetops, up towards the sky
Swinging from branches way up high
Tempt him with a banana or fruit
When he's hungry, he acts so cute!

Birthdate: August 1, 1998
Price Paid: $__________
Date Purchased: __________
Tag Generation: __________

115

Mystic™

Unicorn · #4007
Issued: June 25, 1994
Retired: May 18, 1999

B

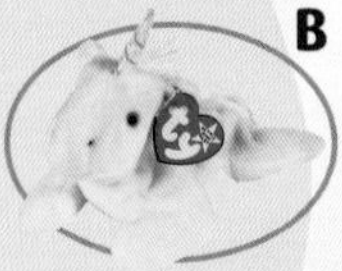

C

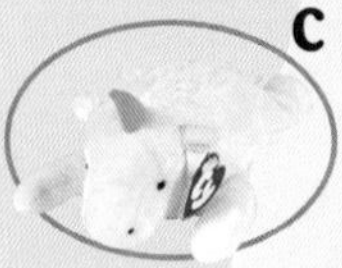

D

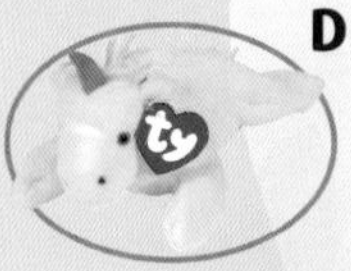

A

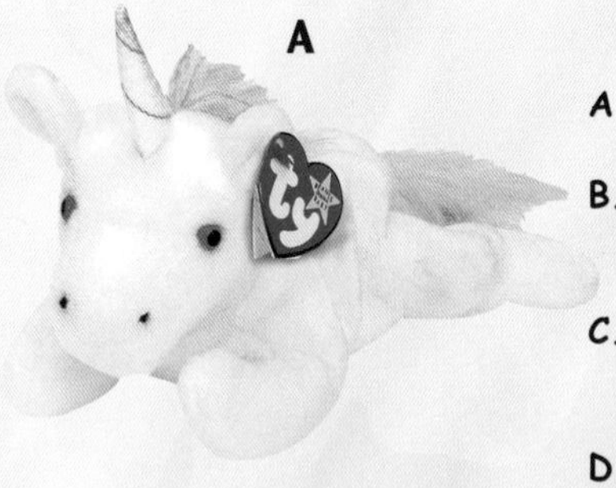

Market Value:
A. Iridescent Horn/Fluffy Mane (Jan. 99-May 99) [5]-$18
B. Iridescent Horn/Coarse Mane (Oct. 97-Dec. 98) [5]-$13 [4]-$16
C. Brown Horn/Coarse Mane (Est. Late 95-Oct. 97) [4]-$32 [3]-$125
D. Brown Horn/Fine Mane (Est. June 94-Late 95) [3]-$320 [2]-$450 [1]-$525

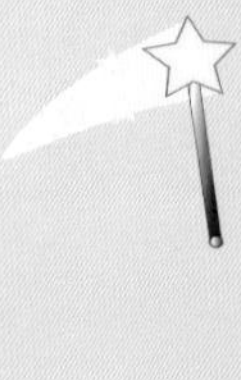

Once upon a time so far away
A unicorn was born one day in May
Keep Mystic with you, she's a prize
You'll see the magic in her blue eyes!

Birthdate: May 21, 1994
Price Paid: $__________
Date Purchased: __________
Tag Generation: __________

Value Totals: __________

116

Nana™

(name changed to "Bongo™")

Monkey · #4067
Issued: June 3, 1995
Retired: 1995

Market Value:
❸- $4,000

Birthdate: N/A
Price Paid: $_____
Date Purchased: _____
Tag Generation: _____

No Poem_____
_____
_____

117

Nanook™

Husky · #4104
Issued: May 11, 1997
Retired: March 31, 1999

Market Value:
❺- $12
❹- $14

Birthdate: November 21, 1996
Price Paid: $_____
Date Purchased: _____
Tag Generation: _____

Nanook is a dog that loves cold weather
To him a sled is light as a feather
Over the snow and through the slush
He runs at hearing the cry of "mush"!

118

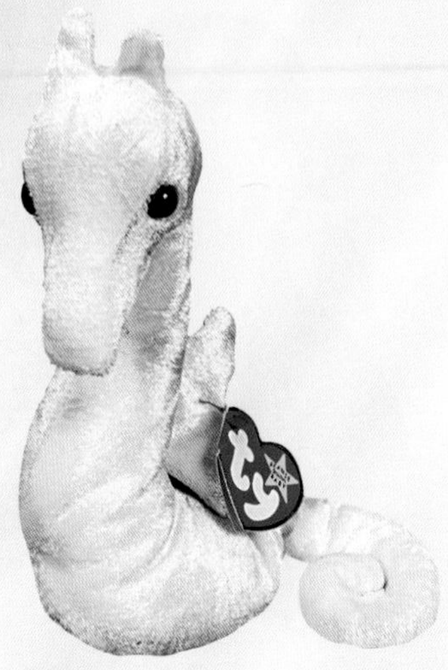

Neon™

Seahorse · #4239
Issued: April 8, 1999
Current – Moderate To Find

Market Value:
[5]- $_____

Born in shallow water in a sea grass bay
Their eyes can swivel and look every way
Walk down the beach on a bright sunny day
Jump into the sea and watch them play!

Birthdate: April 1, 1999
Price Paid: $__________
Date Purchased: __________
Tag Generation: __________

119

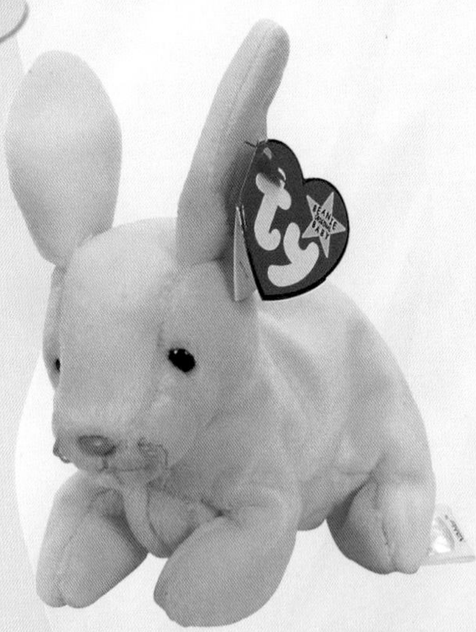

Nibbler™

Rabbit · #4216
Issued: January 1, 1999
Retired: July 9, 1999

Market Value:
[5]- $15

Twitching her nose, she looks so sweet
Small in size, she's very petite
Soft and furry, hopping with grace
She'll visit your garden, her favorite place!

Birthdate: April 6, 1998
Price Paid: $__________
Date Purchased: __________
Tag Generation: __________

Value Totals: __________

120

Nibbly™

Rabbit · #4217
Issued: January 1, 1999
Retired: July 20, 1999

Market Value:
[5]-$14

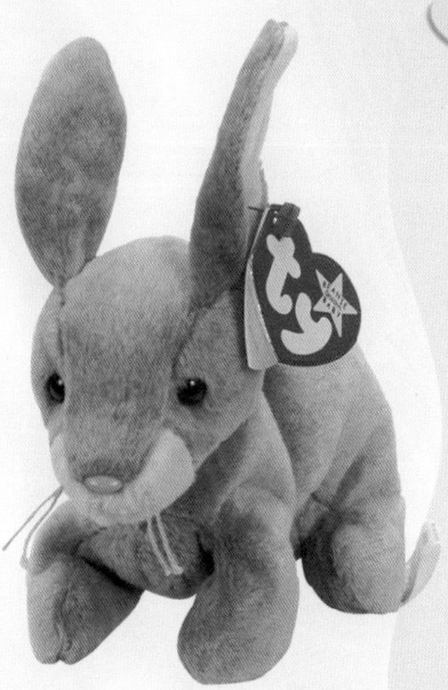

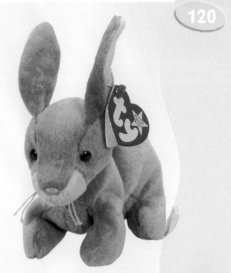

Birthdate: May 7, 1998
Price Paid: $__________
Date Purchased: __________
Tag Generation: __________

Wonderful ways to spend a day
Bright and sunny in the month of May
Hopping around as trees sway
Looking for friends, out to play!

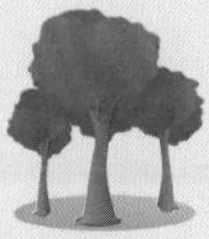

121

Nip™

Cat · #4003
Issued: January 7, 1995
Retired: December 31, 1997

Market Value:
A. White Paws
(March 96-Dec. 97)
[5]-$23 [4]-$23 [3]-$285
B. All Gold
(Jan. 96–March 96)
[3]-$850
C. White Face
(Jan. 95–Jan. 96)
[3]-$500 [2]-$525

A

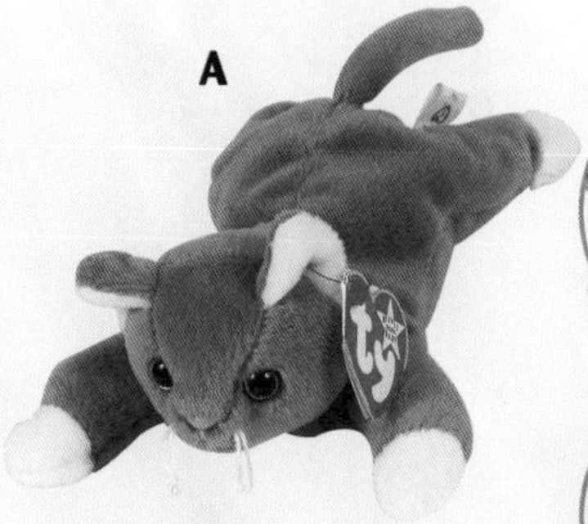

B

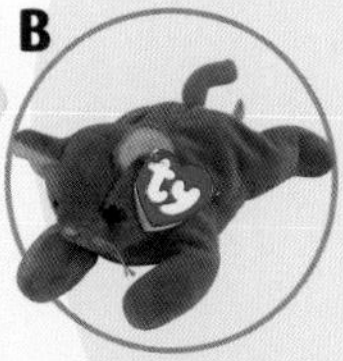

C

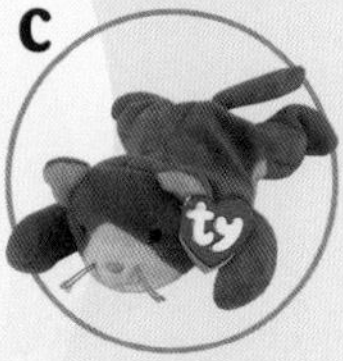

Birthdate: March 6, 1994
Price Paid: $__________
Date Purchased: __________
Tag Generation: __________

His name is Nipper, but we call him Nip
His best friend is a black cat named Zip
Nip likes to run in races for fun
He runs so fast he's always number one!

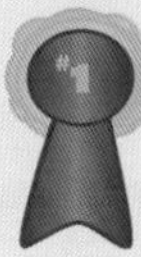

Value Totals: __________

122

Nuts™

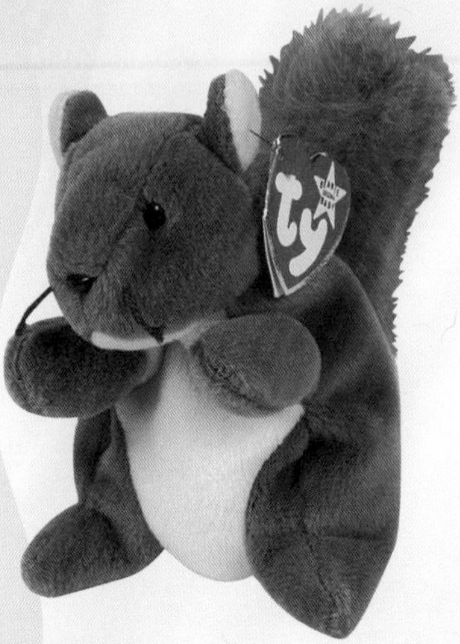

Squirrel · #4114
Issued: January 1, 1997
Retired: December 31, 1998

Market Value:
[5]- $13
[4]- $15

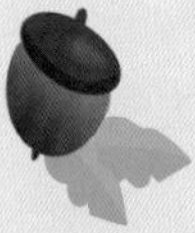

With his bushy tail, he'll scamper up a tree
The most cheerful critter you'll ever see,
He's nuts about nuts, and he loves to chat
Have you ever seen a squirrel like that?

Birthdate: January 21, 1996
Price Paid: $__________
Date Purchased: __________
Tag Generation: __________

123

Osito™

(exclusive to the United States)

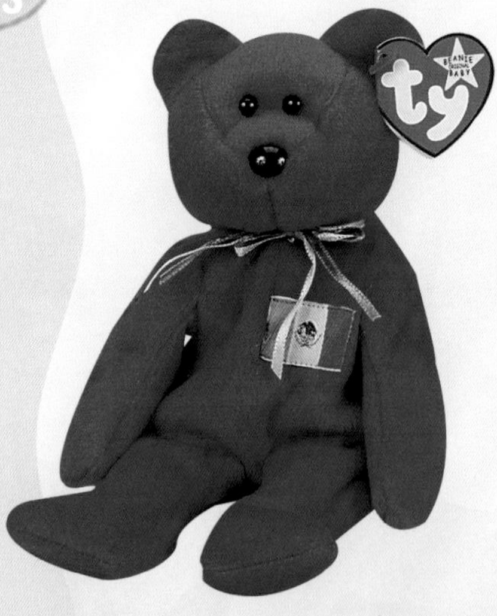

Bear · #4244
Issued: April 17, 1999
Current - Very Hard To Find

Market Value:
[5]- $_____

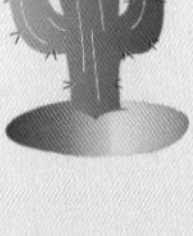

Across the waters of the Rio Grande
Lies a beautiful and mystic land
A place we all should plan to go
Known by all as Mexico!

Birthdate: February 5, 1999
Price Paid: $__________
Date Purchased: __________
Tag Generation: __________

Value Totals: __________

Patti™

124

Platypus • #4025
Issued: January 8, 1994
Retired: May 1, 1998

Market Value:
A. Magenta (Feb. 95-May 98)
[5]-$23
[4]-$26
[3]-$205
B. Maroon (Jan. 94-Feb. 95)
[3]-$670
[2]-$800
[1]-$880

A

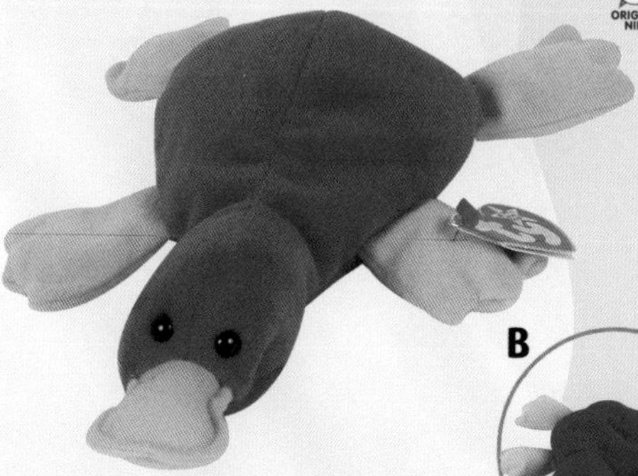

B

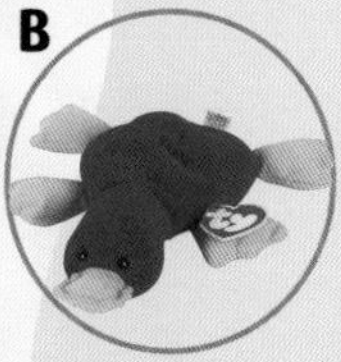

Birthdate: January 6, 1993
Price Paid: $__________
Date Purchased: __________
Tag Generation: __________

Ran into Patti one day while walking
Believe me she wouldn't stop talking
Listened and listened to her speak
That would explain her extra large beak!

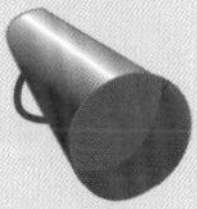

Paul™

125

Walrus • #4248
Issued: April 12, 1999
Current - Moderate To Find

Market Value:
[5]-$_____

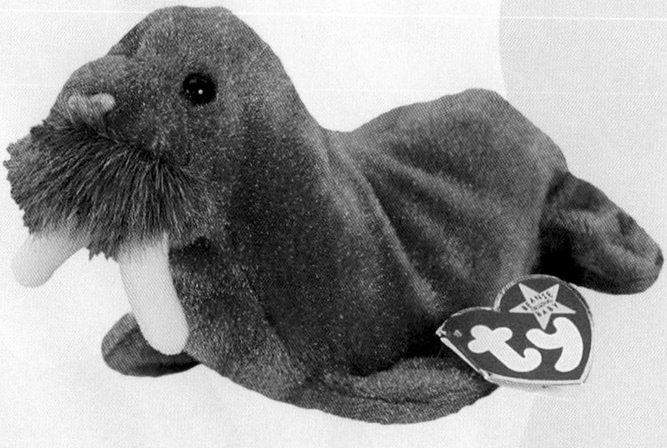

Birthdate: February 23, 1999
Price Paid: $__________
Date Purchased: __________
Tag Generation: __________

Traveling the ocean in a submarine
Singing and playing a tambourine
One day hoping to lead a band
First he needs to find dry land!

126

Peace™

Bear · #4053
Issued: May 11, 1997
Retired: July 14, 1999

Market Value:
[5]-$25
[4]-$35

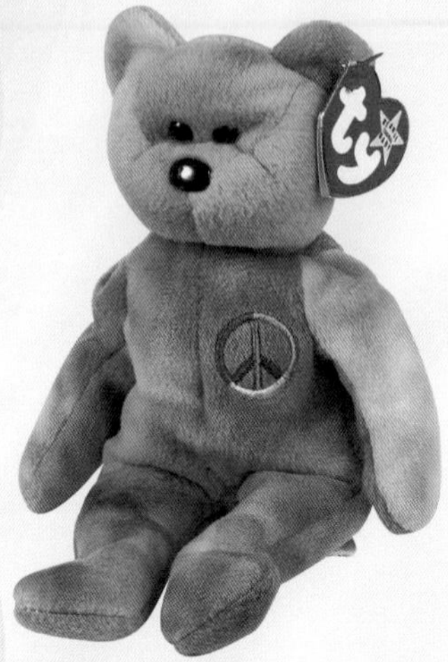

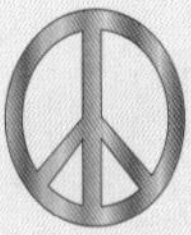

All races, all colors, under the sun
Join hands together and have some fun
Dance to the music, rock and roll is the sound
Symbols of peace and love abound!

Birthdate: February 1, 1996
Price Paid: $__________
Date Purchased: __________
Tag Generation: __________

127

Peanut™

Elephant · #4062
Issued: June 3, 1995
Retired: May 1, 1998

B

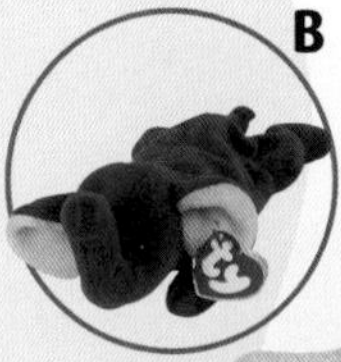

A

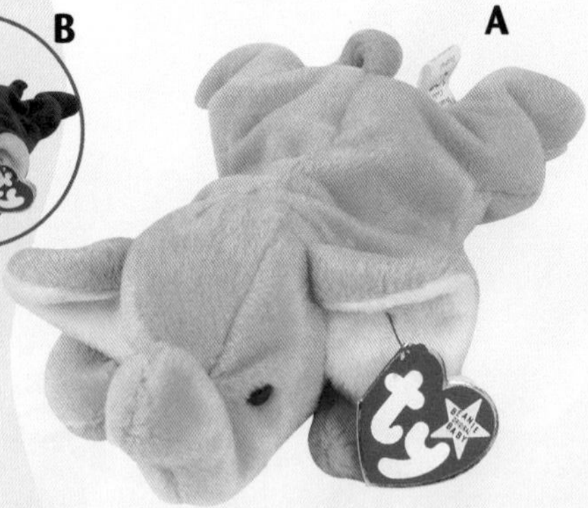

Market Value:
A. Light Blue
(Oct. 95-May 98)
[5]-$21
[4]-$24
[3]-$850
B. Dark Blue
(June 95-Oct. 95)
[3]-$4,700

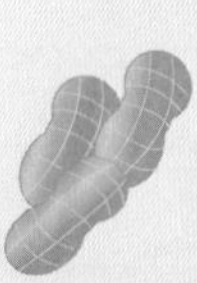

Peanut the elephant walks on tip-toes
Quietly sneaking wherever she goes
She'll sneak up on you and a hug
You will get
Peanut is a friend you won't soon forget!

Birthdate: January 25, 1995
Price Paid: $__________
Date Purchased: __________
Tag Generation: __________

Value Totals: __________

128

Pecan™

Bear · #4251
Issued: April 8, 1999
Current - Moderate To Find

Market Value:
[5]- $_____

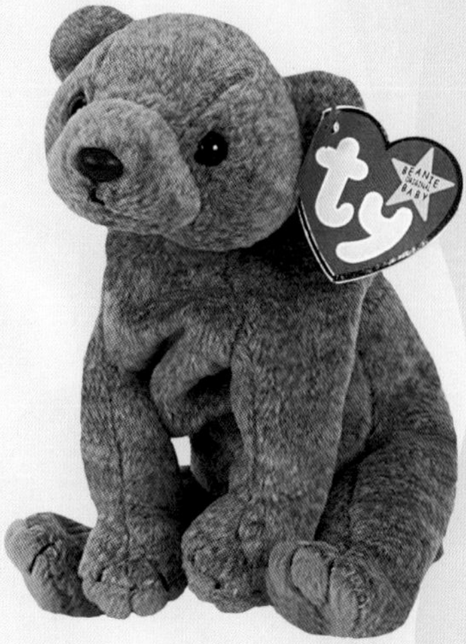

Birthdate: April 15, 1999
Price Paid: $__________
Date Purchased: __________
Tag Generation: __________

In late fall, as wind gusts blow
Pecan hibernates before winter snow
In early spring, sweet scent of a flower
Wakes her up to take a shower!

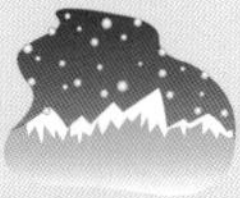

129

Peking™

Panda · #4013
Issued: June 25, 1994
Retired: January 7, 1996

Market Value:
[3]- $1,750
[2]- $1,900
[1]- $2,100

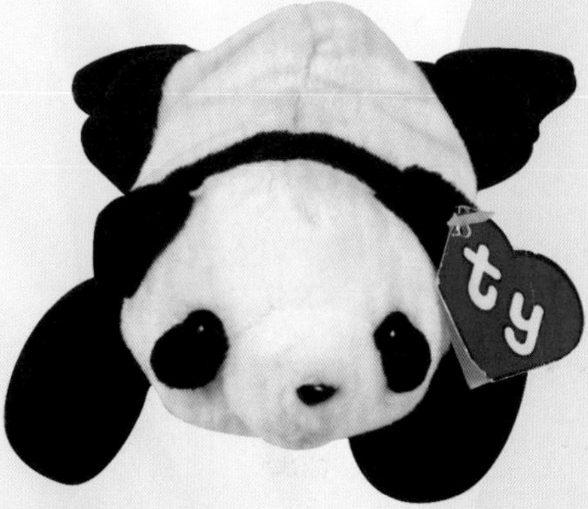

Birthdate: N/A
Price Paid: $__________
Date Purchased: __________
Tag Generation: __________

No Poem__________
____
____
____

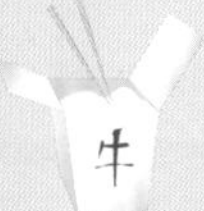

Value Totals: __________

130

ORIGINAL NINE

Pinchers™

Lobster · #4026
Issued: January 8, 1994
Retired: May 1, 1998

B A

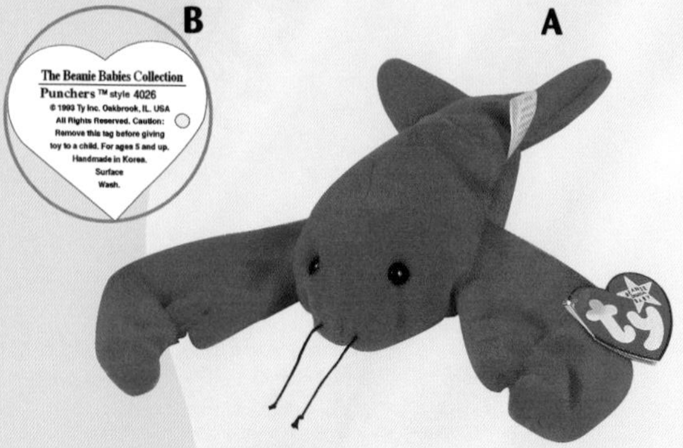

The Beanie Babies Collection
Punchers ™ style 4026
© 1993 Ty Inc. Oakbrook, IL. USA
All Rights Reserved. Caution:
Remove this tag before giving
toy to a child. For ages 5 and up.
Handmade in Korea.
Surface
Wash.
ty

Market Value:
A. "Pinchers™" Swing Tag
(Jan. 94-May 98)
[5]-$23
[4]-$26
[3]-$120
[2]-$400
[1]-$775
B. "Punchers™" Swing Tag
(Est. Early 94)
[1]-$3,400

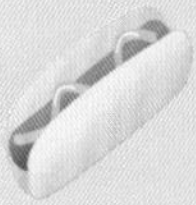

This lobster loves to pinch
Eating his food inch by inch
Balancing carefully with his tail
Moving forward slow as a snail!

Birthdate: June 19, 1993
Price Paid: $__________
Date Purchased: __________
Tag Generation: __________

131

Pinky™

Flamingo · #4072
Issued: June 3, 1995
Retired: December 31, 1998

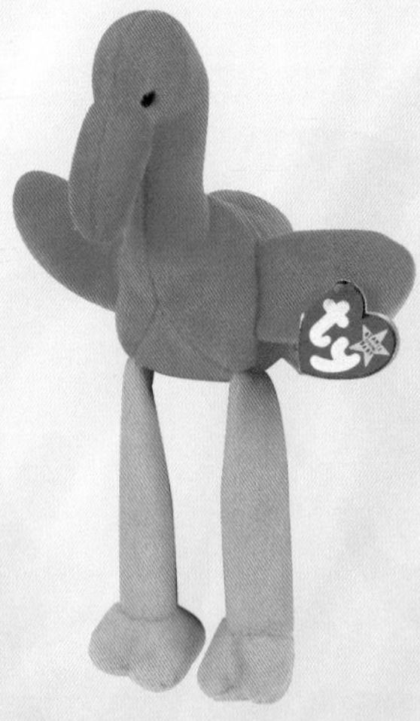

ty

Market Value:
[5]-$12
[4]-$14
[3]-$135

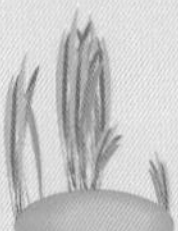

Pinky loves the everglades
From the hottest pink she's made
With floppy legs and big orange beak
She's the Beanie that you seek!

Birthdate: February 13, 1995
Price Paid: $__________
Date Purchased: __________
Tag Generation: __________

Value Totals: __________

132

Pouch™

Kangaroo · #4161
Issued: January 1, 1997
Retired: March 31, 1999

Market Value:
[5]- $11
[4]- $14

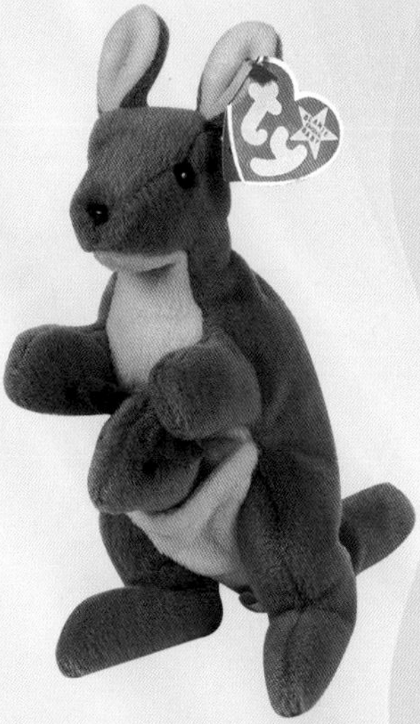

Birthdate: November 6, 1996
Price Paid: $__________
Date Purchased: __________
Tag Generation: __________

My little pouch is handy I've found
It helps me carry my baby around
I hop up and down without any fear
Knowing my baby is safe and near.

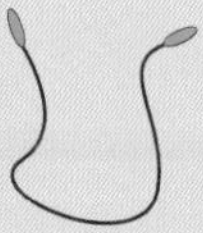

133

Pounce™

Cat · #4122
Issued: December 31, 1997
Retired: March 31, 1999

Market Value:
[5]- $11

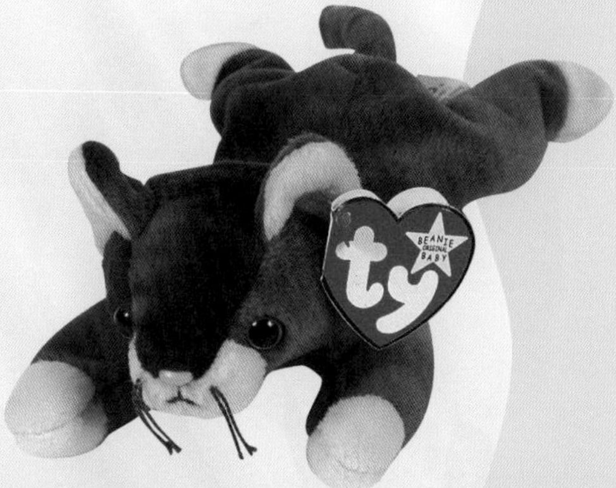

Birthdate: August 28, 1997
Price Paid: $__________
Date Purchased: __________
Tag Generation: __________

Sneaking and slinking down the hall
To pounce upon a fluffy yarn ball
Under the tables, around the chairs
Through the rooms and down the stairs!

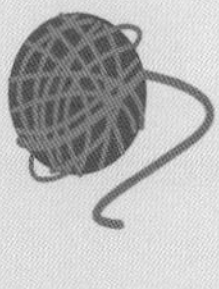

Value Totals: __________

134

Prance™

Cat · #4123
Issued: December 31, 1997
Retired: March 31, 1999

Market Value:
♥5 - $11

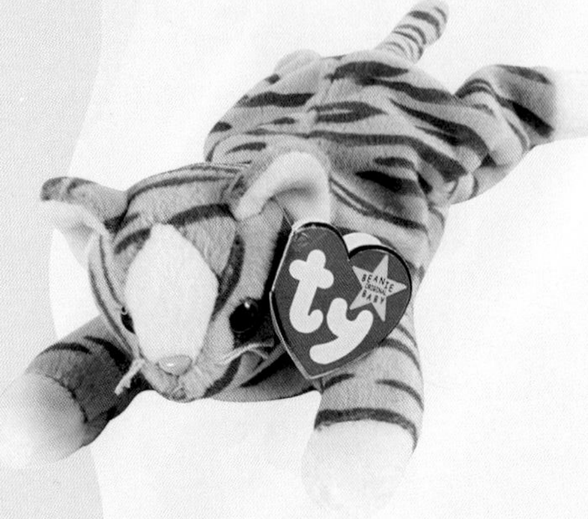

She darts around and swats the air
Then looks confused when nothing's there
Pick her up and pet her soft fur
Listen closely, and you'll hear her purr!

Birthdate: November 20, 1997
Price Paid: $__________
Date Purchased: __________
Tag Generation: __________

135

Prickles™

Hedgehog · #4220
Issued: January 1, 1999
Current - Easy To Find

Market Value:
♥5 - $_____

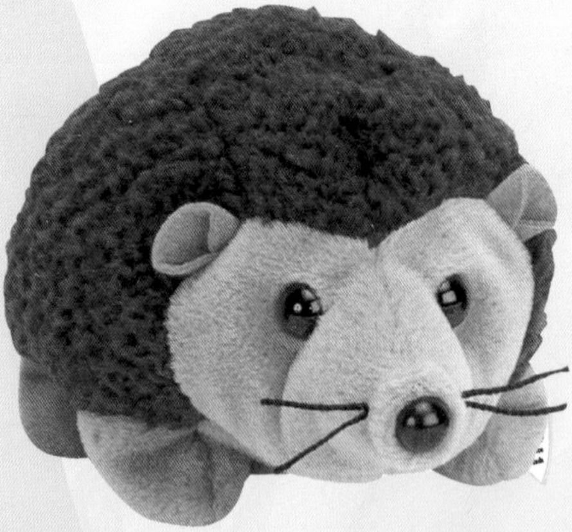

Prickles the hedgehog loves to play
She rolls around the meadow all day
Tucking under her feet and head
Suddenly she looks like a ball instead!

Birthdate: February 19, 1998
Price Paid: $__________
Date Purchased: __________
Tag Generation: __________

Value Totals: __________

Princess™

136

Bear • #4300
Issued: October 29, 1997
Retired: April 13, 1999

Market Value:
A. "P.E. Pellets" On Tush Tag
   (Est. Late 97-April 99)
   ❹- $27
B. "P.V.C. Pellets" On Tush
   Tag (Est. Late 97)
   ❹- $120

A   B

Birthdate: N/A
Price Paid: $_____
Date Purchased: _____
Tag Generation: _____

Like an angel, she came from heaven above
She shared her compassion, her pain, her love
She only stayed with us long enough to teach
The world to share, to give, to reach.

Puffer™

137

Puffin • #4181
Issued: December 31, 1997
Retired: September 18, 1998

Market Value:
❺- $12

Birthdate: November 3, 1997
Price Paid: $_____
Date Purchased: _____
Tag Generation: _____

What in the world does a puffin do?
We're sure that you would like to know too
We asked Puffer how she spends her days
Before she answered, she flew away!

138

Pugsly™

Pug Dog · #4106
Issued: May 11, 1997
Retired: March 31, 1999

Market Value:
[5] - $11
[4] - $13

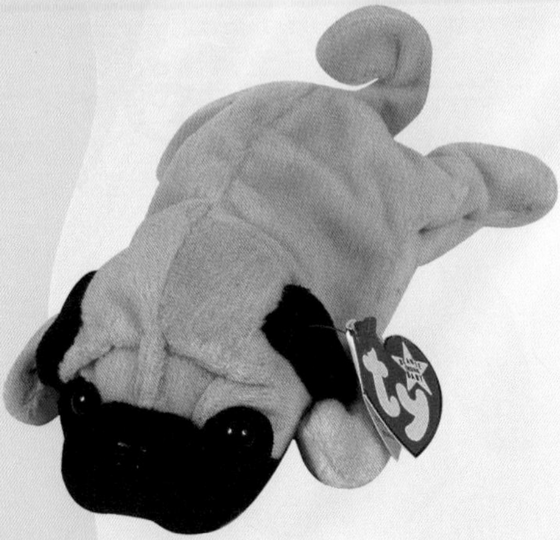

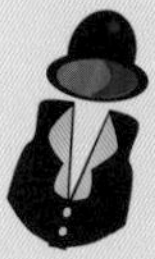

Pugsly is picky about what he will wear
Never a spot, a stain or a tear
Image is something of which he'll gloat
Until he noticed his wrinkled coat!

Birthdate: May 2, 1996
Price Paid: $__________
Date Purchased: __________
Tag Generation: __________

139

Pumkin'™

Pumpkin · #4205
Issued: September 30, 1998
Retired: December 31, 1998

Market Value:
[5] - $32

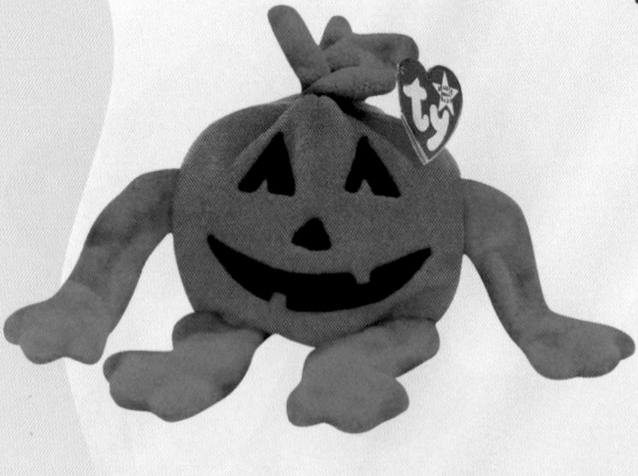

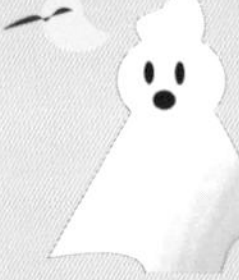

Ghost and goblins are out tonight
Witches try hard to cause fright
This little pumpkin is very sweet
He only wants to trick or treat!

Birthdate: October 31, 1998
Price Paid: $__________
Date Purchased: __________
Tag Generation: __________

Value Totals: __________

140

Quackers™

Duck · #4024
Issued: June 25, 1994
Retired: May 1, 1998

Market Value:
A. "Quackers™" With Wings (Jan. 95-May 98)
5-$17 4-$19
3-$110 2-$700
B. "Quacker™" Without Wings (June 94–Jan. 95)
2-$2,100 1-$2,250

A

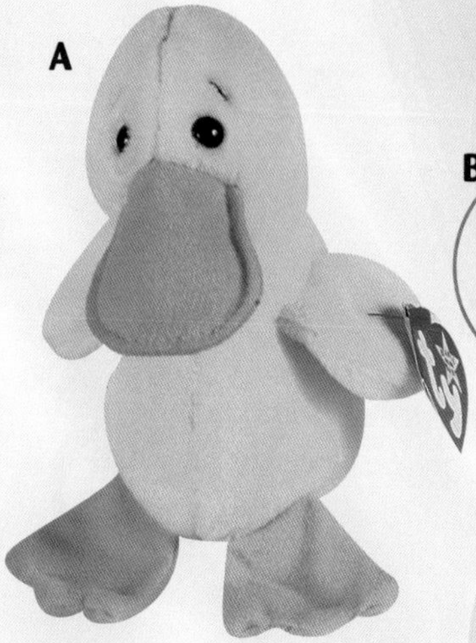

B

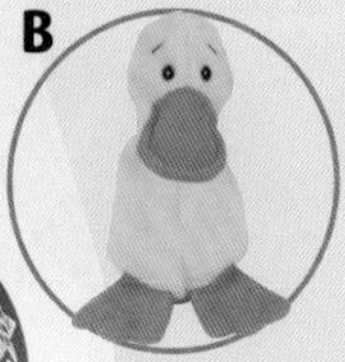

Birthdate: April 19, 1994
Price Paid: $__________
Date Purchased: __________
Tag Generation: __________

There is a duck by the name of Quackers
Every night he eats animal crackers
He swims in a lake that's clear and blue
But he'll come to the shore to be with you!

141

Radar™

Bat · #4091
Issued: September 1, 1995
Retired: May 11, 1997

Market Value:
4-$160
3-$200

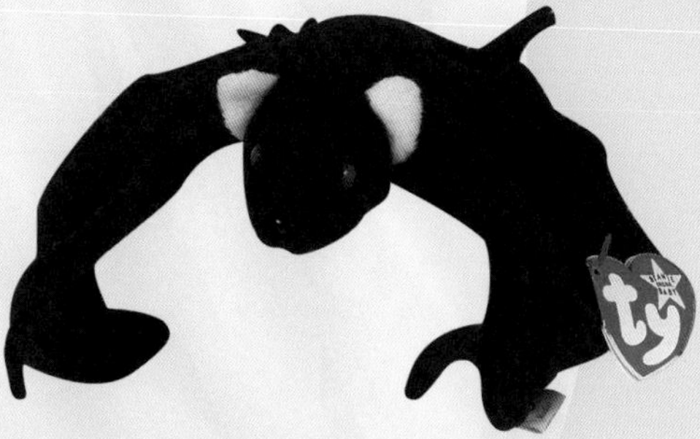

Birthdate: October 30, 1995
Price Paid: $__________
Date Purchased: __________
Tag Generation: __________

Radar the bat flies late at night
He can soar to an amazing height
If you see something as high as a star
Take a good look, it might be Radar!

Value Totals: __________

142

Rainbow™

Chameleon · #4037
Issued: December 31, 1997
Retired: March 31, 1999

B

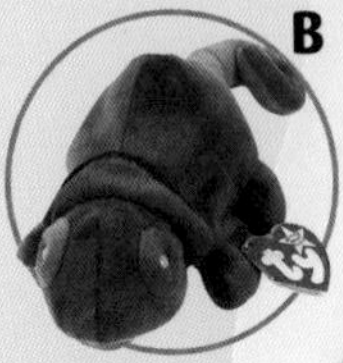

A

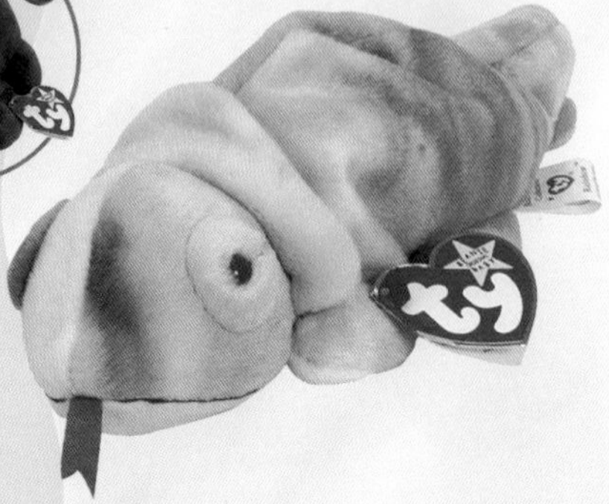

Market Value:
A. Tie-dye/With Tongue
(Mid 98-March 99)
[5]- $14
B. Blue/No Tongue
(Dec. 97-Mid 98)
[5]- $14

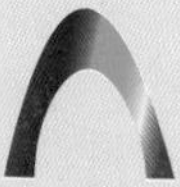

Red, green, blue and yellow
This chameleon is a colorful fellow.
A blend of colors, his own unique hue
Rainbow was made especially for you!

Birthdate: October 14, 1997
Price Paid: $__________
Date Purchased: __________
Tag Generation: __________

143

Rex™

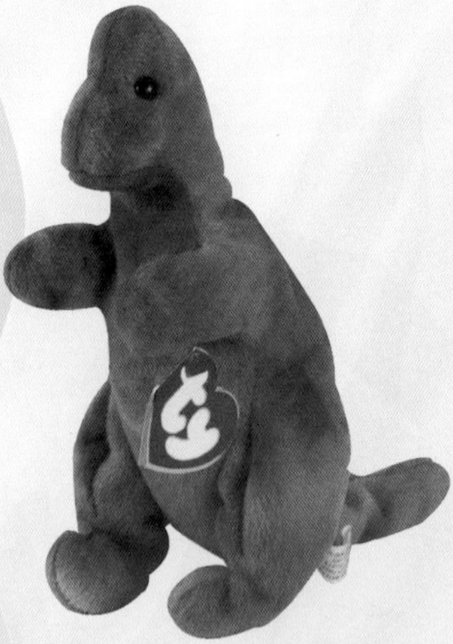

Tyrannosaurus · #4086
Issued: June 3, 1995
Retired: June 15, 1996

Market Value:
[3]- $850

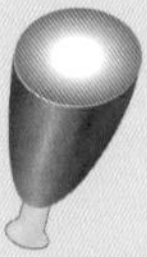

No Poem__________________
____
____
____

Birthdate: N/A
Price Paid: $__________
Date Purchased: __________
Tag Generation: __________

Value Totals: __________

144

Righty™

Elephant · #4086
Issued: June 15, 1996
Retired: January 1, 1997

Market Value:
[4]- $250

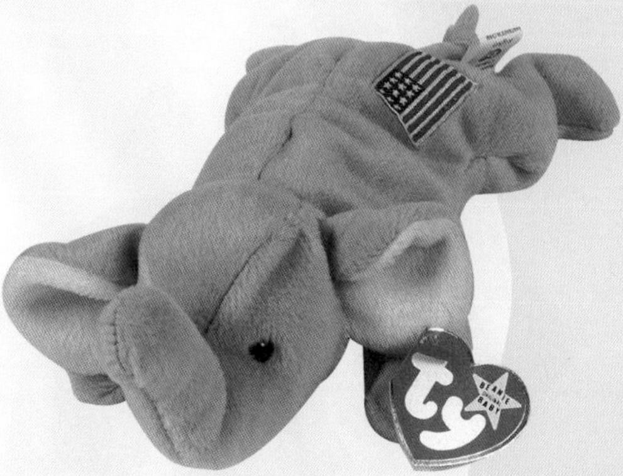

Birthdate: July 4, 1996
Price Paid: $__________
Date Purchased: __________
Tag Generation: __________

Donkeys to the left, elephants to the right
Often seems like a crazy sight
This whole game seems very funny
Until you realize they're spending
Your money!

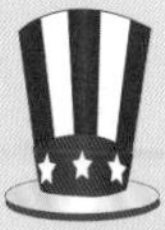

145

Ringo™

Raccoon · #4014
Issued: January 7, 1996
Retired: September 16, 1998

Market Value:
[5]- $14
[4]- $17
[3]- $90

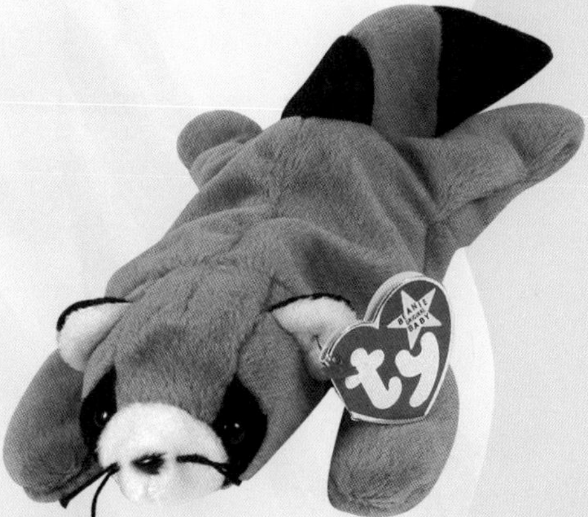

Birthdate: July 14, 1995
Price Paid: $__________
Date Purchased: __________
Tag Generation: __________

Ringo hides behind his mask
He will come out, if you should ask
He loves to chitter. He loves to chatter
Just about anything, it doesn't matter!

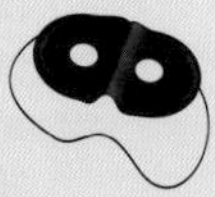

146

Roam™

Buffalo · #4209
Issued: September 30, 1998
Current - Easy To Find

Market Value:
[5]- $_____

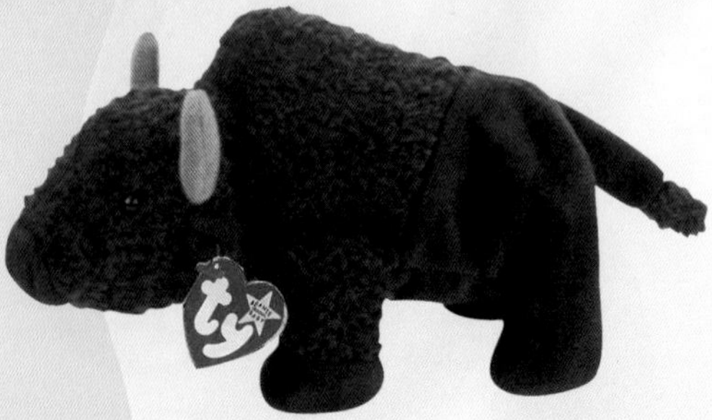

Once roaming wild on American land
Tall and strong, wooly and grand
So rare and special is this guy
Find him quickly, he's quite a buy!

Birthdate: September 27, 1998
Price Paid: $__________
Date Purchased: __________
Tag Generation: __________

147

Roary™

Lion · #4069
Issued: May 11, 1997
Retired: December 31, 1998

Market Value:
[5]- $12
[4]- $14

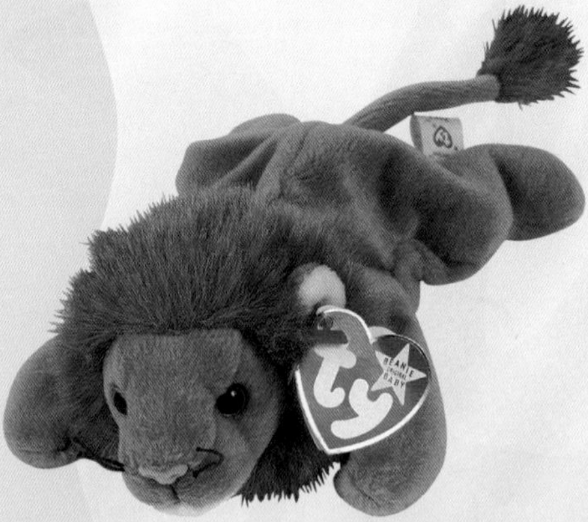

Deep in the jungle they crowned him king
But being brave is not his thing
A cowardly lion some may say
He hears his roar and runs away!

Birthdate: February 20, 1996
Price Paid: $__________
Date Purchased: __________
Tag Generation: __________

Value Totals: __________

148

Rocket™

Blue Jay · #4202
Issued: May 30, 1998
Current - Easy To Find

Market Value:
[5]-$_____

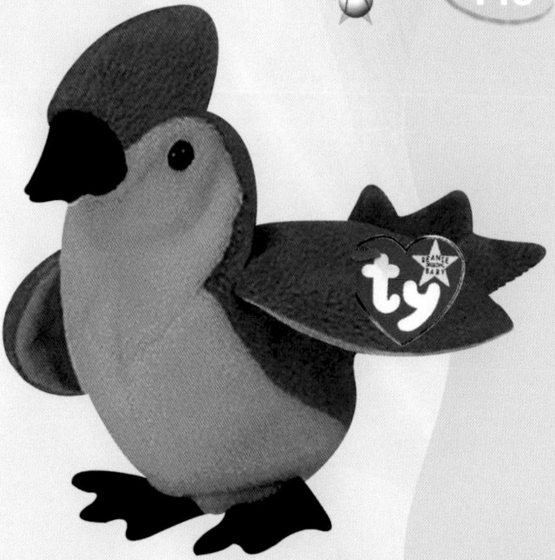

Birthdate: March 12, 1997
Price Paid: $__________
Date Purchased: __________
Tag Generation: __________

Rocket is the fastest blue jay ever
He flies in all sorts of weather
Aerial tricks are his specialty
He's so entertaining for you and me!

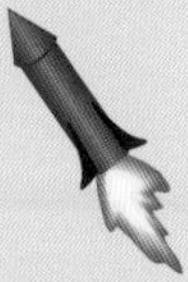

149

Rover™

Dog · #4101
Issued: June 15, 1996
Retired: May 1, 1998

Market Value:
[5]-$24
[4]-$27

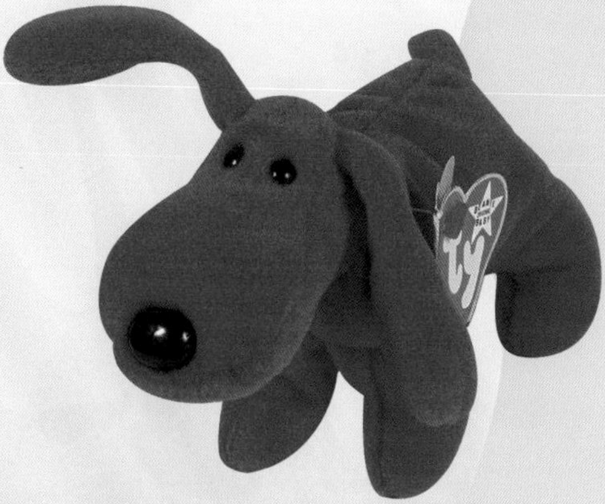

Birthdate: May 30, 1996
Price Paid: $__________
Date Purchased: __________
Tag Generation: __________

This dog is red and his name is Rover
If you call him he is sure to come over
He barks and plays with all his might
But worry not, he won't bite!

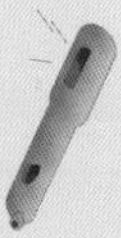

Value Totals: __________

150

Sammy™

Bear · #4215
Issued: January 1, 1999
Current – Moderate To Find

Market Value:
[5]-$_____

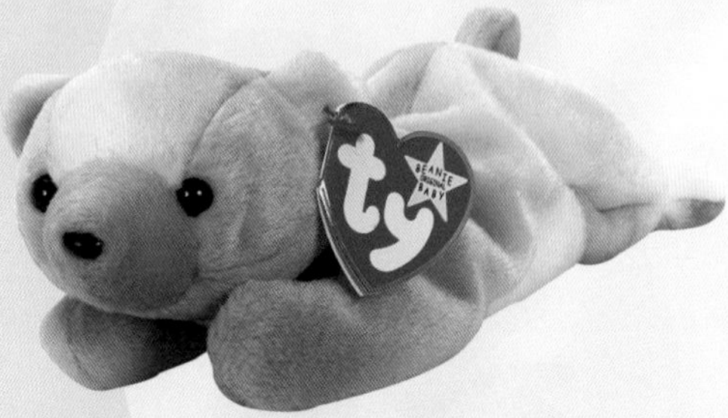

As Sammy steps up to the plate
The crowd gets excited, can hardly wait
We know Sammy won't let us down
He makes us the happiest fans in town!

Birthdate: June 23, 1998
Price Paid: $__________
Date Purchased: __________
Tag Generation: __________

151

Santa™

Santa · #4203
Issued: September 30, 1998
Retired: December 31, 1998

Market Value:
[5]-$34

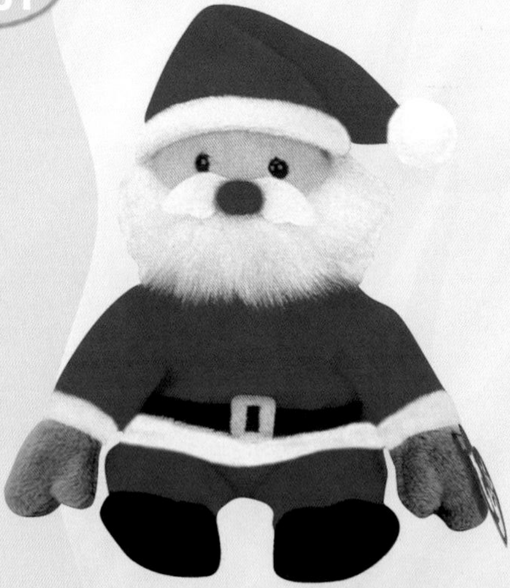

Known by all in his suit of red
Piles of presents on his sled
Generous and giving, he brings us joy
Peace and love, plus this special toy!

Birthdate: December 6, 1998
Price Paid: $__________
Date Purchased: __________
Tag Generation: __________

Value Totals: __________

Scaly™

152

NEW!

Lizard · #4263
Issued: August 31, 1999
Current – Just Released

Market Value:
🖐-$_____

Birthdate: February 9, 1999
Price Paid: $_____
Date Purchased: _____
Tag Generation: _____

I love to lie, basking in the sun
Living in the desert sure is fun
Climbing up cactus, avoiding a spike
I'm the Beanie you're sure to like!

Scat™

153

Cat · #4231
Issued: January 1, 1999
Current – Easy To Find

Market Value:
🖐-$_____

Birthdate: May 27, 1998
Price Paid: $_____
Date Purchased: _____
Tag Generation: _____

Newborn kittens require lots of sleep
Shhh...it's naptime, don't make a peep
Touch her fur, it feels like silk
Wake her up to drink mother's milk!

COLLECTOR'S
VALUE GUIDE™

154

Schweetheart™

Orangutan · #4252
Issued: April 11, 1999
Current – Hard To Find

Market Value:
❺-$_____

Of all the jungles filled with vines
Traveling about, you came to mine
Because of all the things you said
I can't seem to get you otta my head!

Birthdate: January 23, 1999
Price Paid: $_____
Date Purchased: _____
Tag Generation: _____

155

Scoop™

Pelican · #4107
Issued: June 15, 1996
Retired: December 31, 1998

Market Value:
❺-$12
❹-$15

All day long he scoops up fish
To fill his bill, is his wish
Diving fast and diving low
Hoping those fish are very slow!

Birthdate: July 1, 1996
Price Paid: $_____
Date Purchased: _____
Tag Generation: _____

Value Totals: _____

COLLECTOR'S
VALUE GUIDE™

156

Scorch™

Dragon · #4210
Issued: September 30, 1998
Current – Easy To Find

Market Value:
[5]- $_____

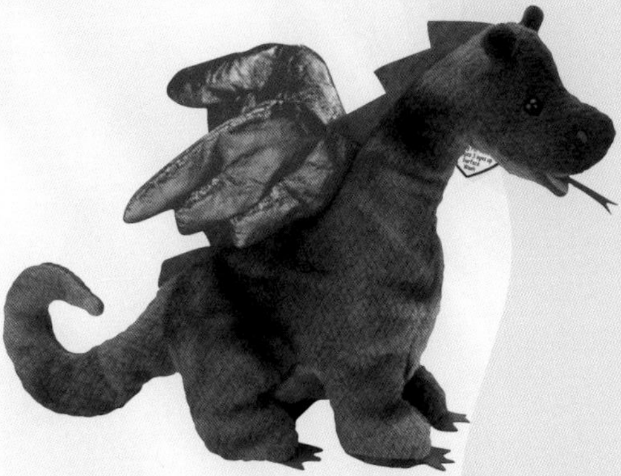

Birthdate: July 31, 1998
Price Paid: $__________
Date Purchased: __________
Tag Generation: __________

A magical mystery with glowing wings
Made by wizards and other things
Known to breathe fire with lots of smoke
Scorch is really a friendly ol' bloke!

157

Scottie™

Scottish Terrier · #4102
Issued: June 15, 1996
Retired: May 1, 1998

Market Value:
[5]- $24
[4]- $27

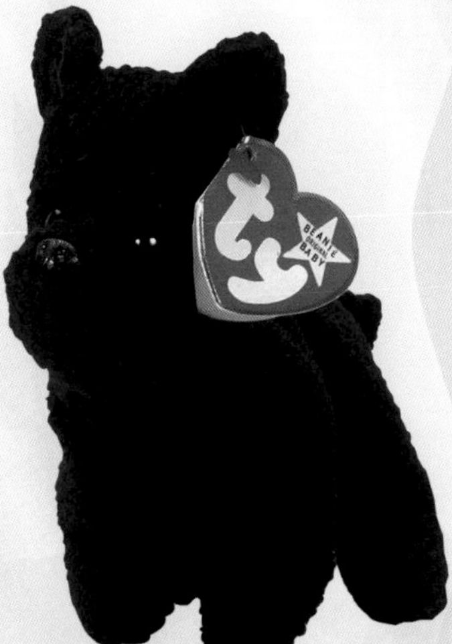

Birthdate: June 3, 1996
or June 15, 1996
Price Paid: $__________
Date Purchased: __________
Tag Generation: __________

Scottie is a friendly sort
Even though his legs are short
He is always happy as can be
His best friends are you and me!

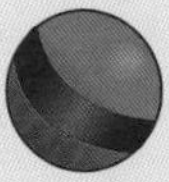

Value Totals: __________

158

Seamore™

Seal · #4029
Issued: June 25, 1994
Retired: October 1, 1997

Market Value:
- **4** - $135
- **3** - $190
- **2** - $395
- **1** - $580

Birthdate: December 14, 1996
Price Paid: $_____
Date Purchased: _____
Tag Generation: _____

Seamore is a little white seal
Fish and clams are her favorite meal
Playing and laughing in the sand
She's the happiest seal in the land!

159

Seaweed™

Otter · #4080
Issued: January 7, 1996
Retired: September 19, 1998

Market Value:
- **5** - $24
- **4** - $28
- **3** - $95

Birthdate: March 19, 1996
Price Paid: $_____
Date Purchased: _____
Tag Generation: _____

Seaweed is what she likes to eat
It's supposed to be a delicious treat
Have you tried a treat from the water
If you haven't, maybe you "otter"!

Value
Totals: _____

COLLECTOR'S
VALUE GUIDE™

Sheets™

160

NEW!

Ghost · #4260
Issued: August 31, 1999
Current – Just Released

Market Value:
[5]-$_____

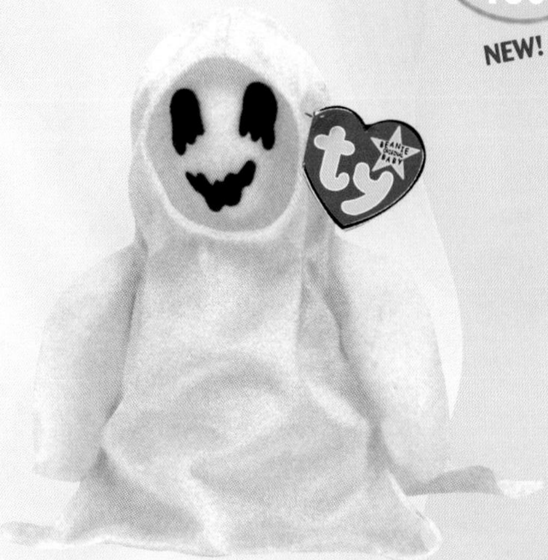

Birthdate: October 31, 1999
Price Paid: $__________
Date Purchased: __________
Tag Generation: __________

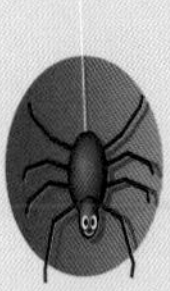

Living alone in a haunted house
Friend to the spider, bat and mouse
Often heard, but never seen
Waiting to wish you "Happy Halloween!"

Silver™

161

Cat · #4242
Issued: April 21, 1999
Current – Easy To Find

Market Value:
[5]-$_____

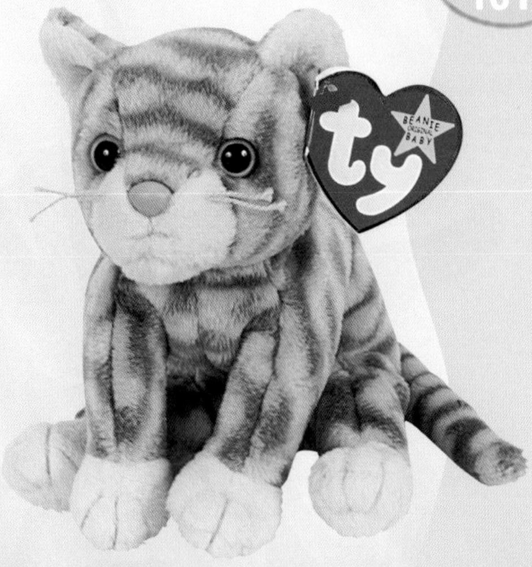

Birthdate: February 11, 1999
Price Paid: $__________
Date Purchased: __________
Tag Generation: __________

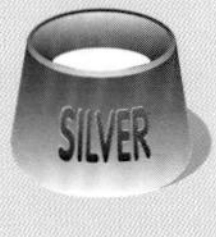

Curled up, sleeping in the sun
He's worn out from having fun
Chasing dust specks in the sunrays
This is how he spends his days!

162

Slippery™

Seal · #4222
Issued: January 1, 1999
Current – Easy To Find

Market Value:
5 – $_____

In the ocean, near a breaking wave
Slippery the seal acts very brave
On his surfboard, he sees a swell
He's riding the wave! Ooooops...he fell!

Birthdate: January 17, 1998
Price Paid: $_____
Date Purchased: _____
Tag Generation: _____

163

Slither™

Snake · #4031
Issued: June 25, 1994
Retired: June 15, 1995

Market Value:
3 – $1,800
2 – $2,000
1 – $2,100

No Poem_____
_____
_____
_____

Birthdate: N/A
Price Paid: $_____
Date Purchased: _____
Tag Generation: _____

Value Totals: _____

COLLECTOR'S
VALUE GUIDE™

Slowpoke™

164

NEW!

Sloth · #4261
Issued: August 31, 1999
Current – Just Released

Market Value:
[5]- $_____

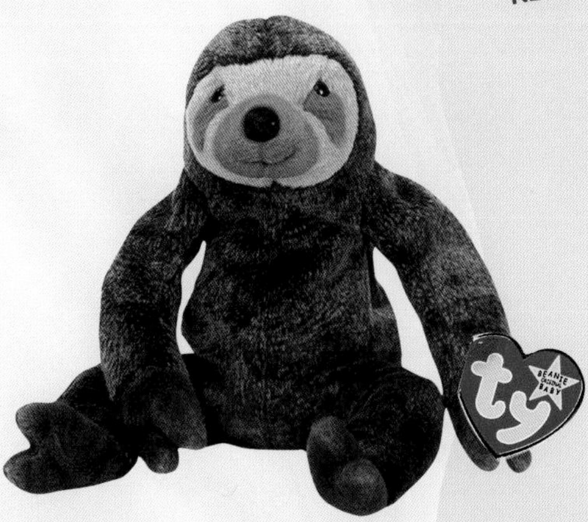

Birthdate: May 20, 1999
Price Paid: $__________
Date Purchased: __________
Tag Generation: __________

Look up in the sky to the top of the tree
What in the world is that you see?
A little sloth as sweet as can be
Munching on leaves very slowly!

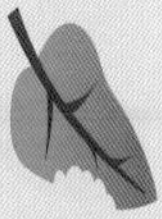

Sly™

165

Fox · #4115
Issued: June 15, 1996
Retired: September 22, 1998

Market Value:
A. White Belly
(Aug. 96-Sept. 98)
[5]- $13
[4]- $16
B. Brown Belly
(June 96-Aug. 96)
[4]- $150

A

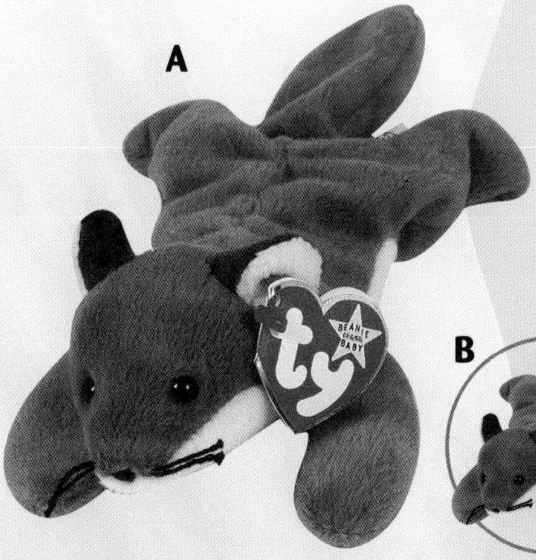

B

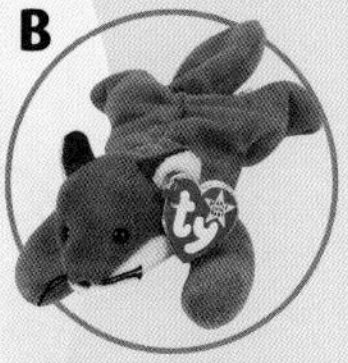

Birthdate: September 12, 1996
Price Paid: $__________
Date Purchased: __________
Tag Generation: __________

Sly is a fox and tricky is he
Please don't chase him, let him be
If you want him, just say when
He'll peek out from his den!

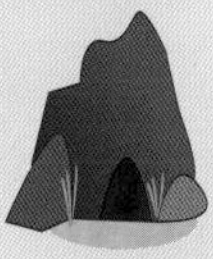

166

Smoochy™

Frog · #4039
Issued: December 31, 1997
Retired: March 31, 1999

Market Value:
❺– $12

Is he a frog or maybe a prince?
This confusion makes him wince
Find the answer, help him with this
Be the one to give him a kiss!

Birthdate: October 1, 1997
Price Paid: $_____
Date Purchased: _____
Tag Generation: _____

167

Snip™

Siamese Cat · #4120
Issued: January 1, 1997
Retired: December 31, 1998

Market Value:
❺– $13
❹– $16

Snip the cat is Siamese
She'll be your friend if you please
So toss her a toy or a piece of string
Playing with you is her favorite thing!

Birthdate: October 22, 1996
Price Paid: $_____
Date Purchased: _____
Tag Generation: _____

Value
Totals: _____

COLLECTOR'S
VALUE GUIDE™

Snort™

Bull · #4002
Issued: January 1, 1997
Retired: September 15, 1998

Market Value:
- 🌀 – $13
- ➍ – $16

Birthdate: May 15, 1995
Price Paid: $_____
Date Purchased: _____
Tag Generation: _____

Although Snort is not so tall
He loves to play basketball
He is a star player in his dreams
Can you guess his favorite team?

Snowball™

Snowman · #4201
Issued: October 1, 1997
Retired: December 31, 1997

Market Value:
- ➍ – $47

Birthdate: December 22, 1996
Price Paid: $_____
Date Purchased: _____
Tag Generation: _____

There is a snowman, I've been told
That plays with Beanies out in the cold
What is better in a winter wonderland
Than a Beanie snowman in your hand!

170

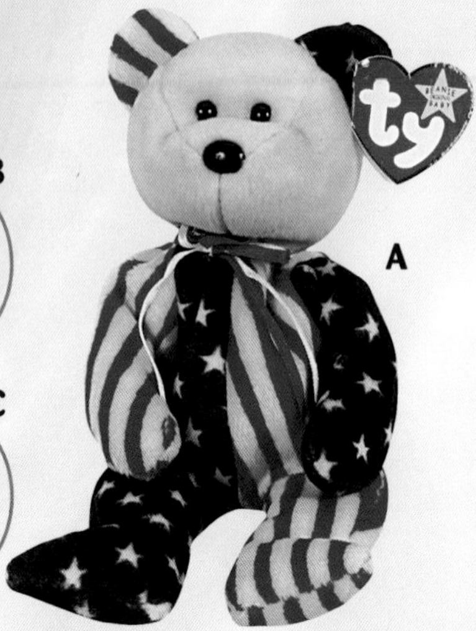

B

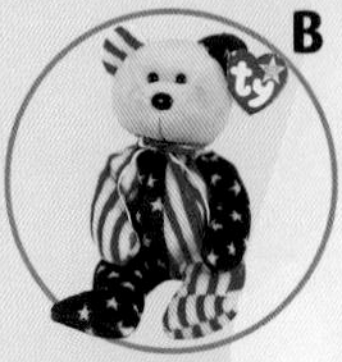

C

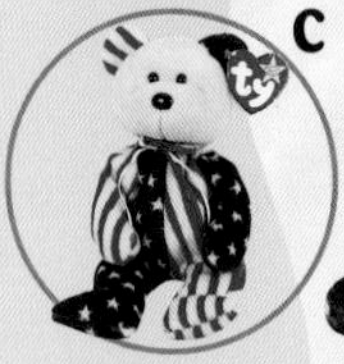

A

Spangle™

Bear · #4245
Issued: April 24, 1999
Current - Very Hard To Find

Market Value:
A. Blue Face
(April 99-Current)
[5]-$_____
B. Red Face
(April 99-Current)
[5]-$_____
C. White Face
(April 99-Current)
[5]-$_____

Stars and stripes he wears proudly
Everywhere he goes he says loudly
"Hip hip hooray, for the land of the free
There's no place on earth I'd rather be!"

Birthdate: June 14, 1999
Price Paid: $__________
Date Purchased: __________
Tag Generation: __________

171

Sparky™

Dalmatian · #4100
Issued: June 15, 1996
Retired: May 11, 1997

Market Value:
[4]-$125

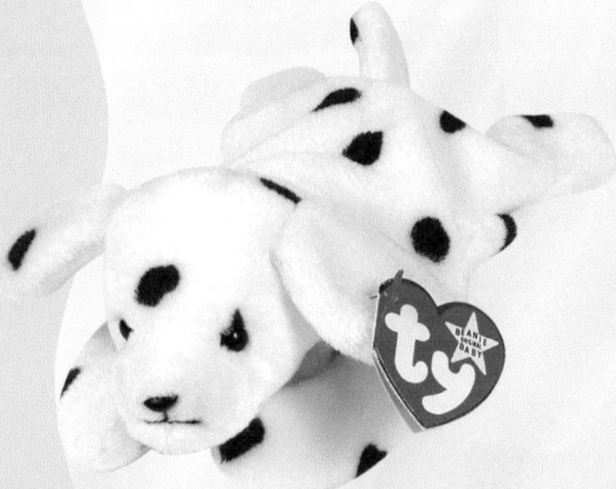

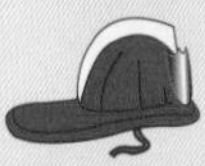

Sparky rides proud on the fire truck
Ringing the bell and pushing his luck
He gets under foot when trying to help
He often gets stepped on and
Lets out a yelp!

Birthdate: February 27, 1996
Price Paid: $__________
Date Purchased: __________
Tag Generation: __________

Value Totals: __________

172

Speedy™

Turtle · #4030
Issued: June 25, 1994
Retired: October 1, 1997

Market Value:
[4]- $35
[3]- $110
[2]- $250
[1]- $425

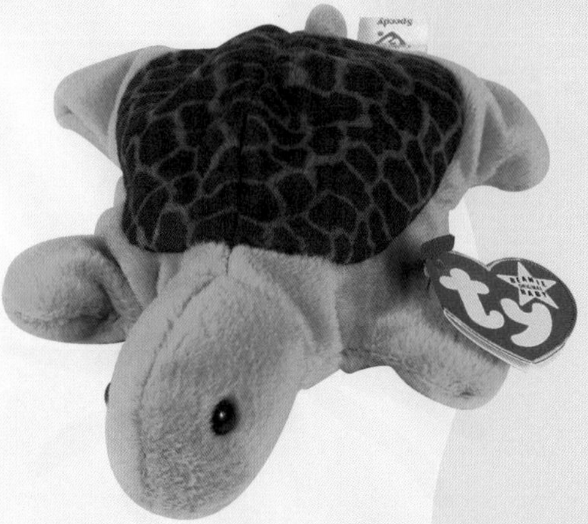

Birthdate: August 14, 1994
Price Paid: $__________
Date Purchased: __________
Tag Generation: __________

Speedy ran marathons in the past
Such a shame, always last
Now Speedy is a big star
After he bought a racing car!

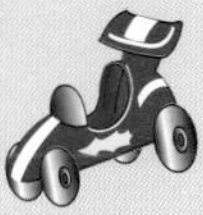

173

Spike™

Rhinoceros · #4060
Issued: June 15, 1996
Retired: December 31, 1998

Market Value:
[5]- $11
[4]- $14

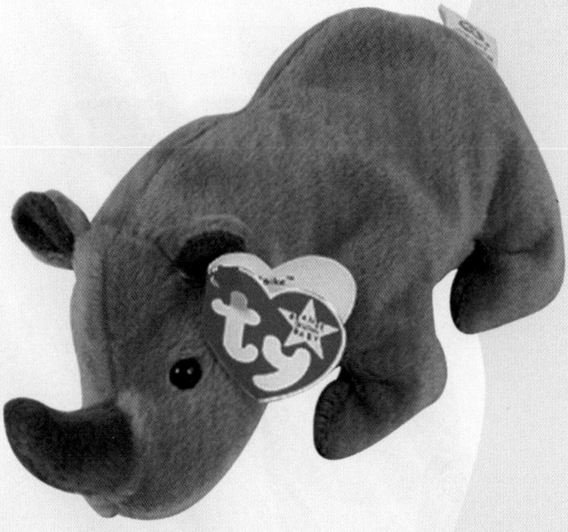

Birthdate: August 13, 1996
Price Paid: $__________
Date Purchased: __________
Tag Generation: __________

Spike the rhino likes to stampede
He's the bruiser that you need
Gentle to birds on his back and spike
You can be his friend if you like!

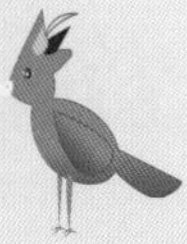

Value Totals: __________

174

Spinner™

Spider · #4036
Issued: October 1, 1997
Retired: September 19, 1998

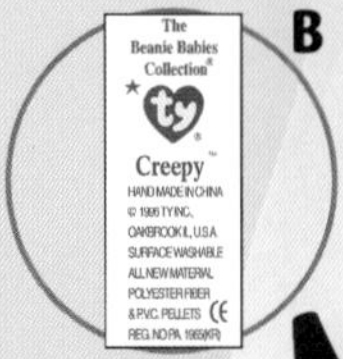

B

A

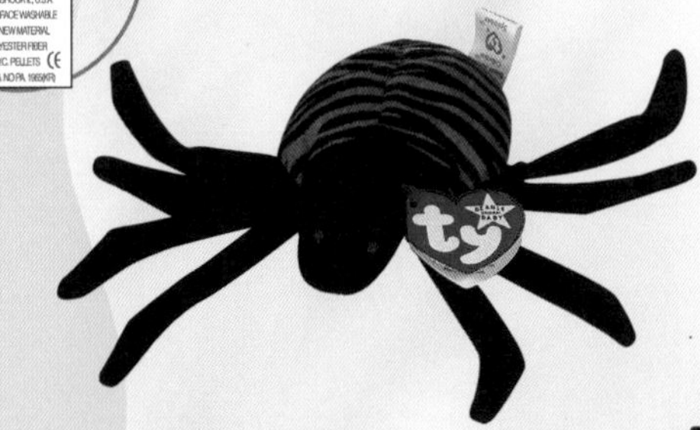

Market Value:
A. "Spinner™" Tush Tag
(Oct. 97-Sept. 98)
[5]- $13
[4]- $17
B. "Creepy™" Tush Tag
(Est. Late 97-Sept. 98)
[5]- $68

Does this spider make you scared?
Among many people that feeling is shared
Remember spiders have feelings too
In fact, this spider really likes you!

Birthdate: October 28, 1996
Price Paid: $__________
Date Purchased: __________
Tag Generation: __________

175

Splash™

ORIGINAL NINE

Whale · #4022
Issued: January 8, 1994
Retired: May 11, 1997

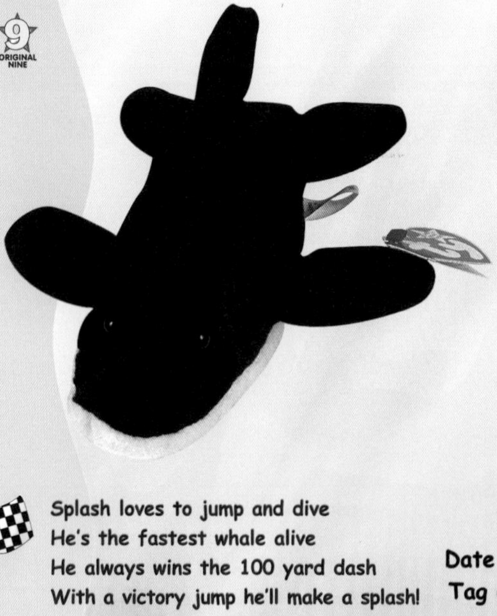

Market Value:
[4]- $130
[3]- $155
[2]- $370
[1]- $535

Splash loves to jump and dive
He's the fastest whale alive
He always wins the 100 yard dash
With a victory jump he'll make a splash!

Birthdate: July 8, 1993
Price Paid: $__________
Date Purchased: __________
Tag Generation: __________

Value Totals: __________

Spooky™

Ghost · #4090
Issued: September 1, 1995
Retired: December 31, 1997

Market Value:
A. "Spooky™" Swing Tag
   (Est. Late 95-Dec. 97)
   ④ - $38
   ❸ - $155
B. "Spook™" Swing Tag
   (Est. Sept. 95-Late 95)
   ❸ - $485

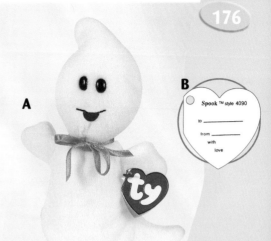

Birthdate: October 31, 1995
Price Paid: $_____
Date Purchased: _____
Tag Generation: _____

Ghosts can be a scary sight
But don't let Spooky bring you any fright
Because when you're alone, you will see
The best friend that Spooky can be!

Spot™

Dog · #4000
Issued: January 8, 1994
Retired: October 1, 1997

Market Value:
A. With Spot
   (April 94-Oct. 97)
   ④ - $55
   ❸ - $135
   ❷ - $670
B. Without Spot
   (Jan. 94-April 94)
   ❷ - $1,800
   ❶ - $2,200

Birthdate: January 3, 1993
Price Paid: $_____
Date Purchased: _____
Tag Generation: _____

See Spot sprint, see Spot run
You and Spot will have lots of fun
Watch out now, because he's not slow
Just stand back and watch him go!

178

Spunky™

Cocker Spaniel · #4184
Issued: December 31, 1997
Retired: March 31, 1999

Market Value:
[5]-$12

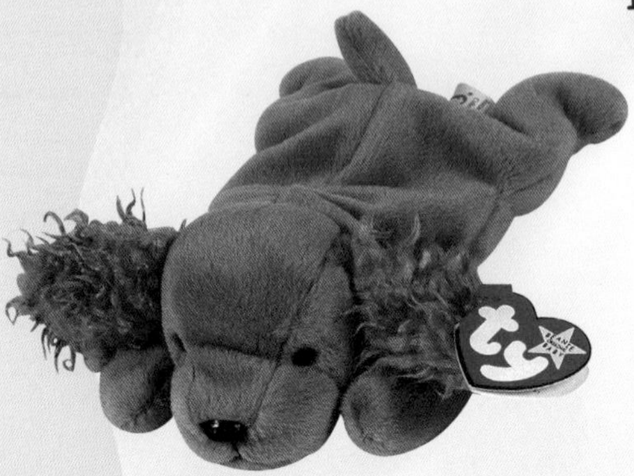

Bouncing around without much grace
To jump on your lap and lick your face
But watch him closely he has no fears
He'll run so fast he'll trip over his ears

Birthdate: January 14, 1997
Price Paid: $________
Date Purchased: ________
Tag Generation: ________

179

ORIGINAL NINE

Squealer™

Pig · #4005
Issued: January 8, 1994
Retired: May 1, 1998

Market Value:
[5]-$29
[4]-$32
[3]-$95
[2]-$280
[1]-$500

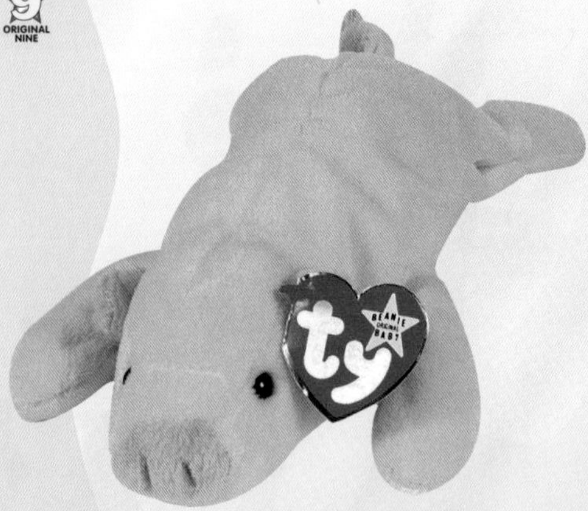

Squealer likes to joke around
He is known as class clown
Listen to his stories awhile
There is no doubt he'll make you smile!

Birthdate: April 23, 1993
Price Paid: $________
Date Purchased: ________
Tag Generation: ________

Value Totals: ________

Steg™

180

Stegosaurus · #4087
Issued: June 3, 1995
Retired: June 15, 1996

Market Value:
❸ – $850

Birthdate: N/A
Price Paid: $_____
Date Purchased: _____
Tag Generation: _____

No Poem_____
_____
_____
_____

Stilts™

181

Stork · #4221
Issued: January 1, 1999
Retired: May 31, 1999

Market Value:
❺ – $12

Birthdate: June 16, 1998
Price Paid: $_____
Date Purchased: _____
Tag Generation: _____

Flying high over mountains and streams
Fulfilling wishes, hopes and dreams
The stork brings parents bundles of joy
The greatest gift, a girl or boy!

COLLECTOR'S
VALUE GUIDE™

Value
Totals: _____

182

Sting™

Stingray · #4077
Issued: June 3, 1995
Retired: January 1, 1997

Market Value:
❹ – $175
❸ – $250

I'm a manta ray and my name is Sting
I'm quite unusual and this is the thing
Under the water I glide like a bird
Have you ever seen something so absurd?

Birthdate: August 27, 1995
Price Paid: $_____
Date Purchased: _____
Tag Generation: _____

183

Stinger™

Scorpion · #4193
Issued: May 30, 1998
Retired: December 31, 1998

Market Value:
❺ – $13

Stinger the scorpion will run and dart
But this little fellow is really all heart
So if you see him don't run away
Say hello and ask him to play!

Birthdate: September 29, 1997
Price Paid: $_____
Date Purchased: _____
Tag Generation: _____

Value
Totals: _____

COLLECTOR'S
VALUE GUIDE™

Stinky™

184

Skunk · #4017
Issued: June 3, 1995
Retired: September 28, 1998

Market Value:
- 5 - $15
- 4 - $18
- 3 - $90

Birthdate: February 13, 1995
Price Paid: $_____
Date Purchased: _____
Tag Generation: _____

Deep in the woods he lived in a cave
Perfume and mints were the gifts he gave
He showered every night in the kitchen sink
Hoping one day he wouldn't stink!

Stretch™

185

Ostrich · #4182
Issued: December 31, 1997
Retired: March 31, 1999

Market Value:
- 5 - $12

Birthdate: September 21, 1997
Price Paid: $_____
Date Purchased: _____
Tag Generation: _____

She thinks when her head is underground
The rest of her body can't be found
The Beanie Babies think it's absurd
To play hide and seek with this bird!

COLLECTOR'S VALUE GUIDE™

Value Totals: _____

186

Stripes™

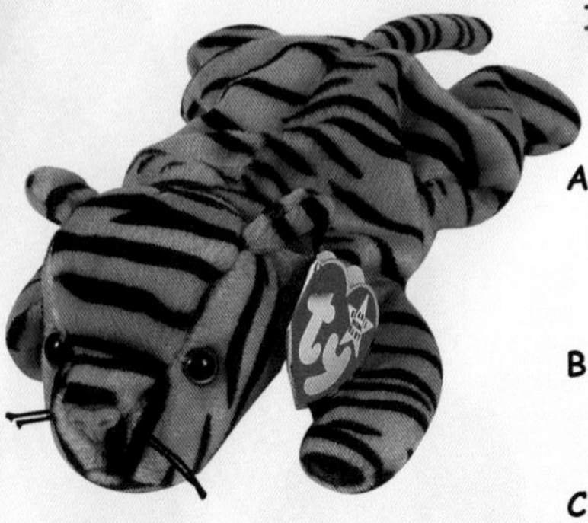

A

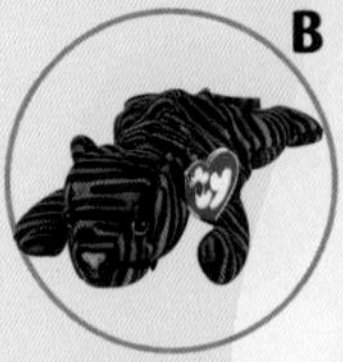

B

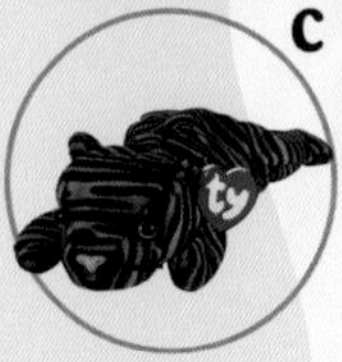

C

Tiger · #4065
Issued: Est. June 3, 1995
Retired: May 1, 1998

Market Value:
A. Light w/Fewer Stripes (June 96-May 98)
[5]-$17
[4]-$20
B. Dark w/Fuzzy Belly (Est. Early 96-June 96)
[3]-$1,000
C. Dark w/More Stripes (Est. June 95-Early 96)
[3]-$400

Birthdate: June 11, 1995
Price Paid: $__________
Date Purchased: __________
Tag Generation: __________

Stripes was never fierce nor strong
So with tigers, he didn't get along
Jungle life was hard to get by
So he came to his friends at Ty!

187

Strut™

(name changed from "Doodle™")

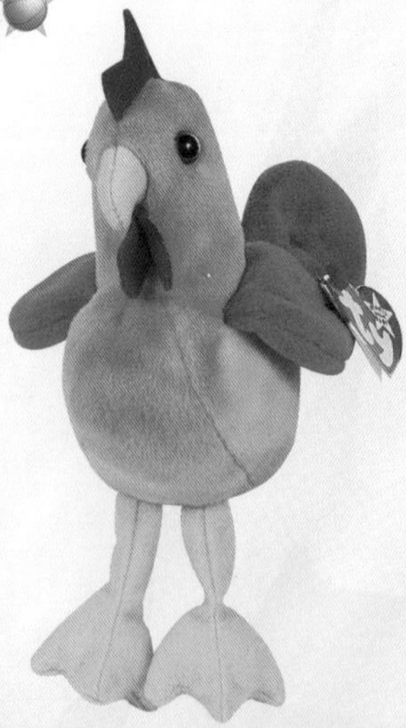

Rooster · #4171
Issued: July 12, 1997
Retired: March 31, 1999

Market Value:
[5]-$12
[4]-$16

Birthdate: March 8, 1996
Price Paid: $__________
Date Purchased: __________
Tag Generation: __________

Listen closely to "cock-a-doodle-doo"
What's the rooster saying to you?
Hurry, wake up sleepy head
We have lots to do, get out of bed!

Value Totals: __________

188

Swirly™

Snail · #4249
Issued: April 14, 1999
Current - Moderate To Find

Market Value:
[5]-$_____

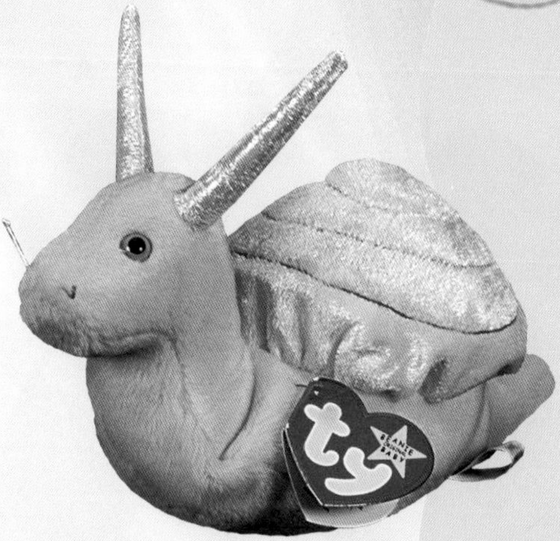

Birthdate: March 10, 1999
Price Paid: $__________
Date Purchased: __________
Tag Generation: __________

Carefully traveling, leaving a trail
I'm not very fast, for I am a snail
Although I go my own plodding pace
Slow and steady, wins the race!

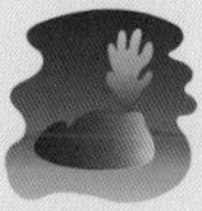

189

Tabasco™

Bull · #4002
Issued: June 3, 1995
Retired: January 1, 1997

Market Value:
[4]-$170
[3]-$225

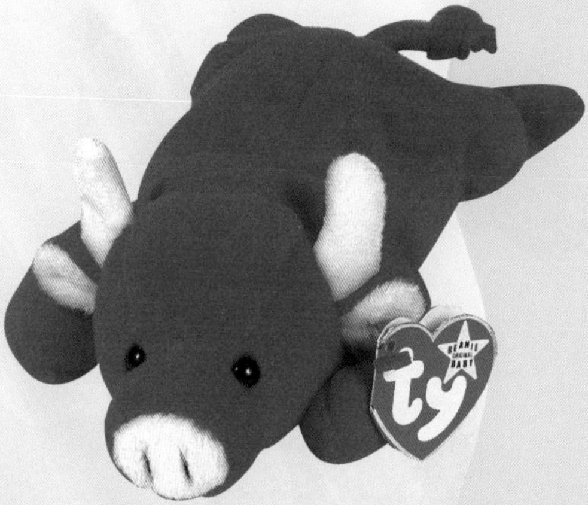

Birthdate: May 15, 1995
Price Paid: $__________
Date Purchased: __________
Tag Generation: __________

Although Tabasco is not so tall
He loves to play basketball
He is a star player in his dream
Can you guess his favorite team?

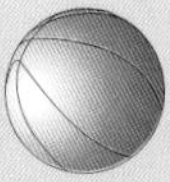

Value Totals: __________

190

Tank™

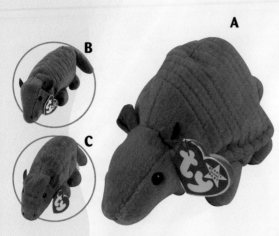

B

C

A

Armadillo · #4031
Issued: Est. January 7, 1996
Retired: October 1, 1997

Market Value:
A. 9 Plates/With Shell
   (Est. Late 96-Oct. 97)
   ❹-$75
B. 9 Plates/Without Shell
   (Est. Mid 96-Late 96)
   ❹-$230
C. 7 Plates/Without Shell
   (Est. Jan 96-Mid 96)
   ❸-$195

This armadillo lives in the South
Shoving Tex-Mex in his mouth
He sure loves it south of the border
Keeping his friends in good order!

Birthdate: February 22, 1995
Price Paid: $_____
Date Purchased: _____
Tag Generation: _____

191

Teddy™ (brown)

B

A

Bear · #4050
Issued: June 25, 1994
Retired: October 1, 1997

Market Value:
A. New Face (Jan. 95-Oct. 97)
   ❹-$95
   ❸-$375
   ❷-$750
B. Old Face (June 94-Jan. 95)
   ❷-$2,400
   ❶-$2,600

Teddy wanted to go out today
All of his friends went out to play
But he'd rather help whatever you do
After all, his best friend is you!

Birthdate: November 28, 1995
Price Paid: $_____
Date Purchased: _____
Tag Generation: _____

Value
Totals: _____

COLLECTOR'S
VALUE GUIDE™

192

Teddy™ (cranberry)

Bear · #4052
Issued: June 25, 1994
Retired: January 7, 1996

Market Value:
A. New Face (Jan. 95-Jan. 96)
   ❸- $1,800
   ❷- $1,900
B. Old Face (June 94-Jan. 95)
   ❷- $1,700
   ❶- $1,800

A

B

Birthdate: N/A
Price Paid: $_____
Date Purchased: _____
Tag Generation: _____

No Poem _____
_____
_____
_____

193

Teddy™ (jade)

Bear · #4057
Issued: June 25, 1994
Retired: January 7, 1996

Market Value:
A. New Face (Jan. 95-Jan. 96)
   ❸- $1,800
   ❷- $1,900
B. Old Face (June 94-Jan. 95)
   ❷- $1,700
   ❶- $1,800

A

B

Birthdate: N/A
Price Paid: $_____
Date Purchased: _____
Tag Generation: _____

No Poem _____
_____
_____
_____

Value
Totals: _____

194

Teddy™ (magenta)

Bear • #4056
Issued: June 25, 1994
Retired: January 7, 1996

Market Value:
A. New Face (Jan. 95-Jan. 96)
❸- $1,800
❷- $1,900
B. Old Face (June 94-Jan. 95)
❷- $1,700
❶- $1,800

Birthdate: N/A
Price Paid: $_____
Date Purchased: _____
Tag Generation: _____

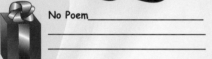

No Poem_____
_____
_____
_____

195

Teddy™ (teal)

Bear • #4051
Issued: June 25, 1994
Retired: January 7, 1996

Market Value:
A. New Face (Jan. 95-Jan. 96)
❸- $1,800
❷- $1,900
B. Old Face (June 94-Jan. 95)
❷- $1,700
❶- $1,800

Birthdate: N/A
Price Paid: $_____
Date Purchased: _____
Tag Generation: _____

No Poem_____
_____
_____
_____

Value Totals: _____

COLLECTOR'S
VALUE GUIDE™

196

Teddy™ (violet)

Bear · #4055
Issued: June 25, 1994
Retired: January 7, 1996

Market Value:
A. New Face (Jan. 95-Jan. 96)
❸- $1,800
❷- $1,900
B. New Face/Employee Bear
w/Red Tush Tag (Green or
Red Ribbon, Sept. 96)
No Swing Tag – $3,800
C. Old Face (June 94-Jan. 95)
❷- $1,700
❶- $1,800

Birthdate: N/A
Price Paid: $_____
Date Purchased: _____
Tag Generation: _____

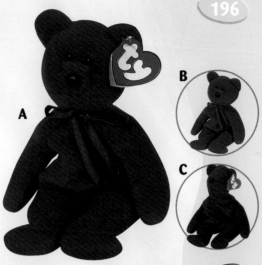

A

B

C

No Poem_____
_____
_____

197

The End™

NEW!

Bear · #4265
Issued: August 31, 1999
Current – Just Released

Market Value:
❺- $_____

Birthdate: N/A
Price Paid: $_____
Date Purchased: _____
Tag Generation: _____

All good things come to an end
It's been fun for everyone
Peace and hope are never gone
Love you all and say, "So long!"

COLLECTOR'S VALUE GUIDE™

Value
Totals: _____

125

198

Tiny™

Chihuahua • #4234
Issued: January 1, 1999
Current – Easy To Find

Market Value:
●-$_____

South of the Border, in the sun
Tiny the Chihuahua is having fun
Attending fiestas, breaking piñatas
Eating a taco, or some enchiladas!

Birthdate: September 8, 1998
Price Paid: $_____
Date Purchased: _____
Tag Generation: _____

199

Tiptoe™

Mouse • #4241
Issued: April 16, 1999
Current – Moderate To Find

Market Value:
●-$_____

Creeping quietly along the wall
Little foot prints fast and small
Tiptoeing through the house with ease
Searching for a piece of cheese!

Birthdate: January 8, 1999
Price Paid: $_____
Date Purchased: _____
Tag Generation: _____

Value
Totals: _____

COLLECTOR'S
VALUE GUIDE™

Tracker™

200

Basset Hound · #4198
Issued: May 30, 1998
Current – Easy To Find

Market Value:
❺- $_____

Birthdate: June 5, 1997
Price Paid: $_____
Date Purchased: _____
Tag Generation: _____

Sniffing and tracking and following trails
Tracker the basset always wags his tail
It doesn't matter what you do
He's always happy when he's with you!

Trap™

201

Mouse · #4042
Issued: June 25, 1994
Retired: June 15, 1995

Market Value:
❸- $1,400
❷- $1,550
❶- $1,700

Birthdate: N/A
Price Paid: $_____
Date Purchased: _____
Tag Generation: _____

No Poem_____
_____
_____
_____

Tuffy™

Terrier · #4108
Issued: May 11, 1997
Retired: December 31, 1998

Market Value:
5 – $12
4 – $15

Taking off with a thunderous blast
Tuffy rides his motorcycle fast
The Beanies roll with laughs and squeals
He never took off his training wheels!

Birthdate: October 12, 1996
Price Paid: $_____
Date Purchased: _____
Tag Generation: _____

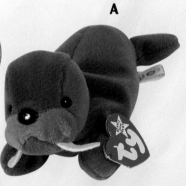

B   **A**

Tuck™ style 4076
DATE OF BIRTH : 9-18-95

Tusk brushes his teeth everyday
To keep them shiny, it's the only way
Teeth are special, so you must try
And they will sparkle when
You say "Hi"!

Visit our web page!!!
http://www.ty.com

Tusk™

Walrus · #4076
Issued: Est. June 3, 1995
Retired: January 1, 1997

Market Value:
A. "Tusk™" Swing Tag
(Est. June 95–Jan. 97)
4 – $125
3 – $180
B. "Tuck™" Swing Tag
(Est. Early 96–Jan. 97)
4 – $145

Tusk brushes his teeth everyday
To keep them shiny, it's the only way
Teeth are special, so you must try
And they will sparkle when
You say "Hi"!

Birthdate: September 18, 1995
Price Paid: $_____
Date Purchased: _____
Tag Generation: _____

Value
Totals: _____

COLLECTOR'S
VALUE GUIDE™

Twigs™

204

Giraffe · #4068
Issued: January 7, 1996
Retired: May 1, 1998

Market Value:
[5]-$23
[4]-$26
[3]-$100

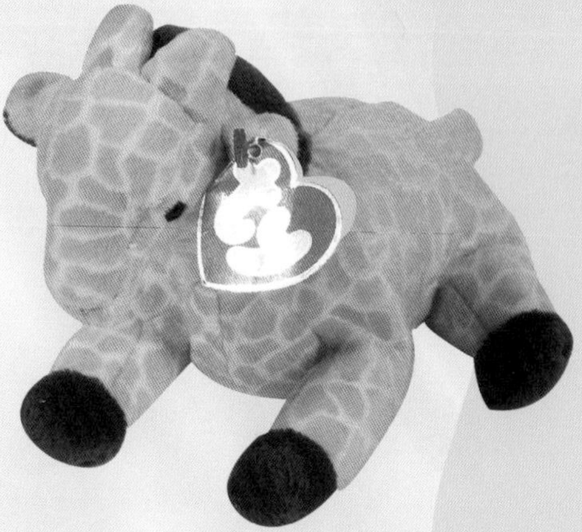

Birthdate: May 19, 1995
Price Paid: $__________
Date Purchased: __________
Tag Generation: __________

Twigs has his head in the clouds
He stands tall, he stands proud
With legs so skinny they wobble and shake
What an unusual friend he will make!

Ty 2K™

205

NEW!

Bear · #4262
Issued: August 31, 1999
Current - Just Released

Market Value:
[5]-$_____

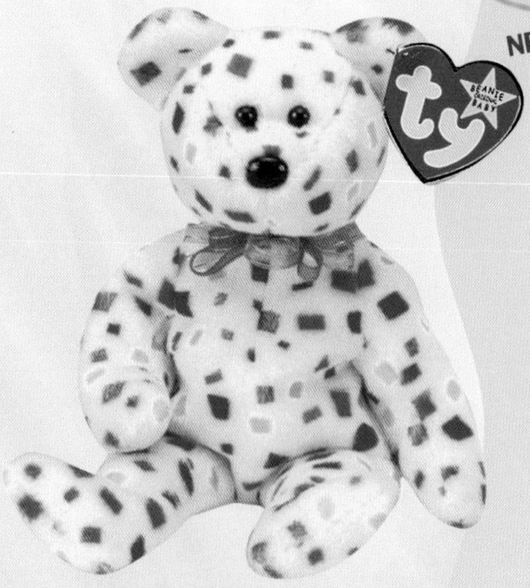

Birthdate: January 1, 2000
Price Paid: $__________
Date Purchased: __________
Tag Generation: __________

Red, yellow, green and blue
Let's have some fun me and you
So join the party, and let's all say
"Happy New Millennium", from Ty 2K!

Value Totals: __________

206

Valentina™

Bear · #4233
Issued: January 1, 1999
Current – Moderate To Find

Market Value:
5 – $_____

Flowers, candy and hearts galore
Sweet words of love for those you adore
With this bear comes love that's true
On Valentine's Day and all year through!

Birthdate: February 14, 1998
Price Paid: $_____
Date Purchased: _____
Tag Generation: _____

207

Valentino™

Bear · #4058
Issued: January 7, 1995
Retired: December 31, 1998

Market Value:
5 – $25
4 – $28
3 – $160
2 – $260

His heart is red and full of love
He cares for you so give him a hug
Keep him close when feeling blue
Feel the love he has for you!

Birthdate: February 14, 1994
Price Paid: $_____
Date Purchased: _____
Tag Generation: _____

Value Totals: _____

COLLECTOR'S
VALUE GUIDE™

Velvet™

208

Panther · #4064
Issued: June 3, 1995
Retired: October 1, 1997

Market Value:
- ❹ – $33
- ❸ – $105

Birthdate: December 16, 1995
Price Paid: $_____
Date Purchased: _____
Tag Generation: _____

Velvet loves to sleep in the trees
Lulled to dreams by the buzz of the bees
She snoozes all day and plays all night
Running and jumping in the moonlight!

Waddle™

209

Penguin · #4075
Issued: June 3, 1995
Retired: May 1, 1998

Market Value:
- ❺ – $24
- ❹ – $27
- ❸ – $105

Birthdate: December 19, 1995
Price Paid: $_____
Date Purchased: _____
Tag Generation: _____

Waddle the Penguin likes to dress up
Every night he wears his tux
When Waddle walks, it never fails
He always trips over his tails!

Value
Totals: _____

210

NEW!

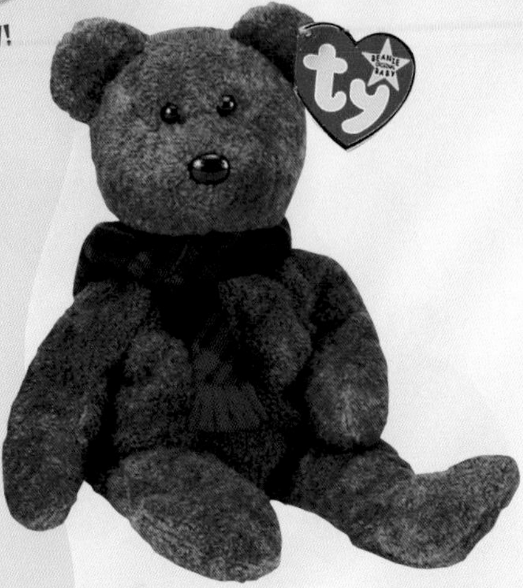

Wallace™

Bear · #4264
Issued: August 31, 1999
Current – Just Released

Market Value:
[5]- $_____

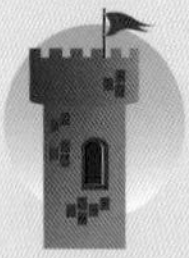

Castles rise from misty glens
Shielding bands of warrior men
Wearing tartan of their clan
Red, green and a little tan!

Birthdate: January 25, 1999
Price Paid: $__________
Date Purchased: __________
Tag Generation: __________

211

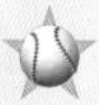

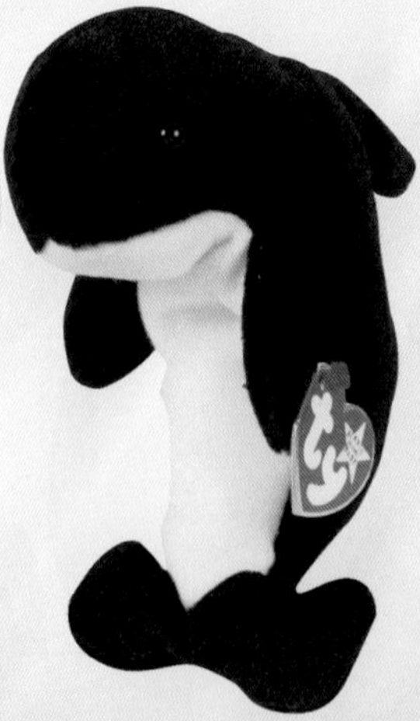

Waves™

Whale · #4084
Issued: May 11, 1997
Retired: May 1, 1998

Market Value:
[5]- $18
[4]- $21

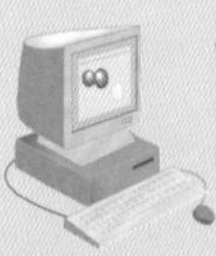

Join him today on the Internet
Don't be afraid to get your feet wet
He taught all the Beanies how to surf
Our web page is his home turf!

Birthdate: December 8, 1996
Price Paid: $__________
Date Purchased: __________
Tag Generation: __________

Value Totals: __________

Web™

212

Spider • #4041
Issued: June 25, 1994
Retired: January 7, 1996

Market Value:
- ❸- $1,200
- ❷- $1,300
- ❶- $1,450

Birthdate: N/A
Price Paid: $_____
Date Purchased: _____
Tag Generation: _____

No Poem_____
_____
_____
_____

Weenie™

 213

Dachshund • #4013
Issued: January 7, 1996
Retired: May 1, 1998

Market Value:
- ❺- $32
- ❹- $35
- ❸- $120

Birthdate: July 20, 1995
Price Paid: $_____
Date Purchased: _____
Tag Generation: _____

Weenie the dog is quite a sight
Long of body and short of height
He perches himself high on a log
And considers himself to be top dog!

TOP DOG

Value
Totals: _____

214

Whisper™

Deer · #4194
Issued: May 30, 1998
Current - Easy To Find

Market Value:
[5]-$_____

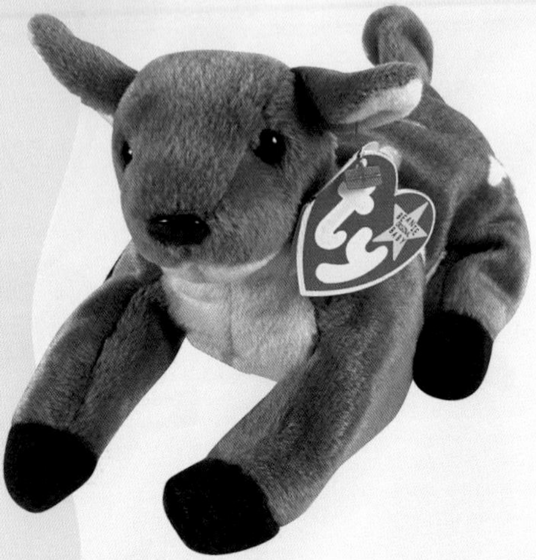

She's very shy as you can see
When she hides behind a tree
With big brown eyes and soft to touch
This little fawn will love you so much!

Birthdate: April 5, 1997
Price Paid: $__________
Date Purchased: __________
Tag Generation: __________

215

Wise™

Owl · #4187
Issued: May 30, 1998
Retired: December 31, 1998

Market Value:
[5]-$30

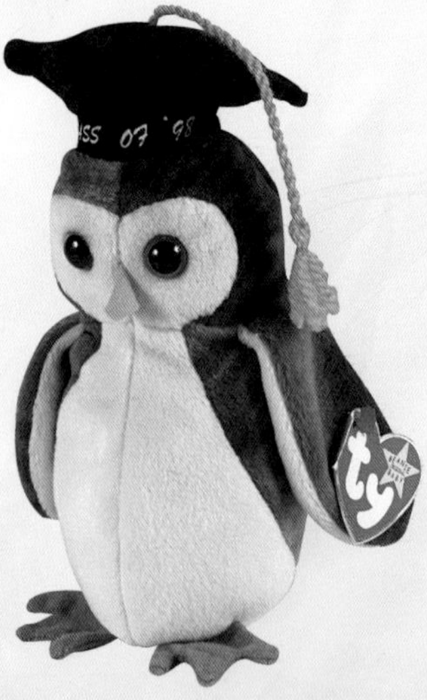

Wise is at the head of the class
With A's and B's he'll always pass
He's got his diploma and feels really great
Meet the newest graduate: Class of '98!

Birthdate: May 31, 1997
Price Paid: $__________
Date Purchased: __________
Tag Generation: __________

Value Totals: __________

216

Wiser™

Owl · #4238
Issued: April 22, 1999
Retired: August 27, 1999

Market Value:
[5]- $25

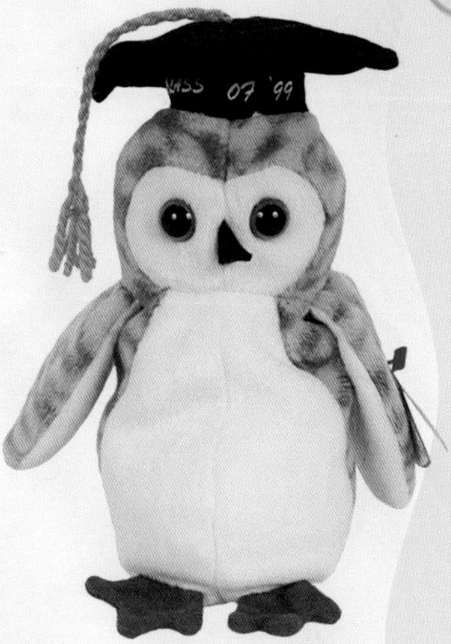

Birthdate: June 4, 1999
Price Paid: $__________
Date Purchased: __________
Tag Generation: __________

Waking daily to the morning sun
Learning makes school so much fun
Looking great and feeling fine
The newest graduate, "Class of 99!"

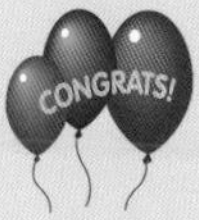

217

Wrinkles™

Bulldog · #4103
Issued: June 15, 1996
Retired: September 22, 1998

Market Value:
[5]- $14
[4]- $17

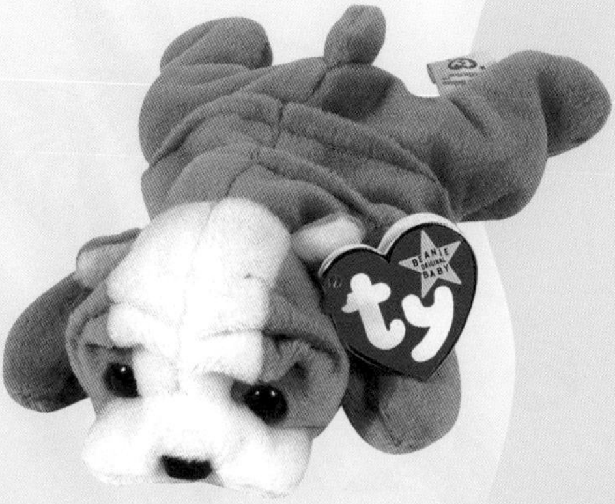

Birthdate: May 1, 1996
Price Paid: $__________
Date Purchased: __________
Tag Generation: __________

This little dog is named Wrinkles
His nose is soft and often crinkles
Likes to climb up on your lap
He's a cheery sort of chap!

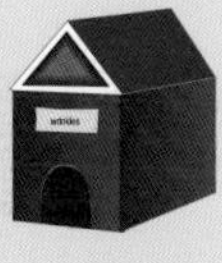

218

Zero™

Penguin · #4207
Issued: September 30, 1998
Retired: December 31, 1998

Market Value:
[5] - $30

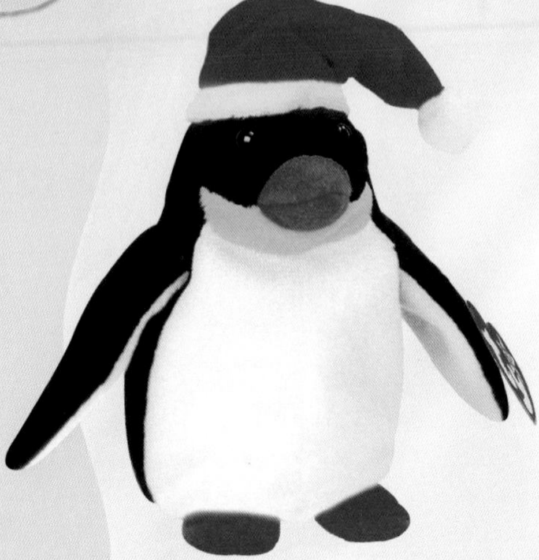

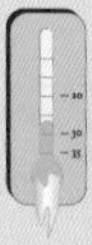

Penguins love the ice and snow
Playing in weather twenty below
Antarctica is where I love to be
Splashing in the cold, cold sea!

Birthdate: January 2, 1998
Price Paid: $__________
Date Purchased: __________
Tag Generation: __________

219

Ziggy™

Zebra · #4063
Issued: June 3, 1995
Retired: May 1, 1998

Market Value:
[5] - $23
[4] - $25
[3] - $95

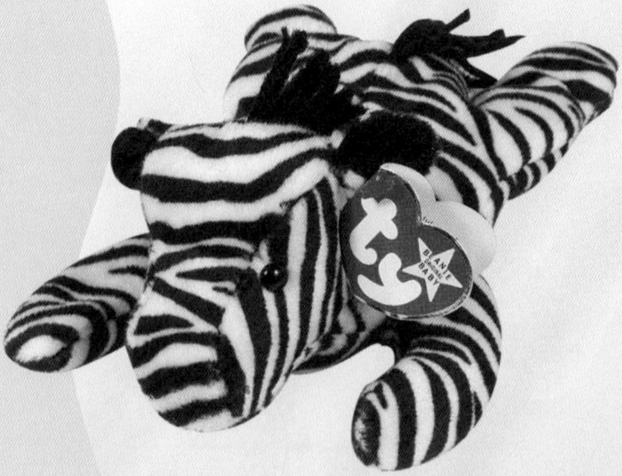

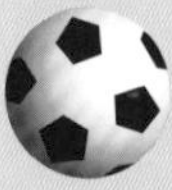

Ziggy likes soccer - he's a referee
That way he watches the games for free
The other Beanies don't think it's fair
But Ziggy the Zebra doesn't care!

Birthdate: December 24, 1995
Price Paid: $__________
Date Purchased: __________
Tag Generation: __________

Value Totals: __________

Zip™

Cat • #4004
Issued: January 7, 1995
Retired: May 1, 1998

Market Value:

A. White Paws
(March 96-May 98)
[5]-$37 [4]-$40 [3]-$360

B. All Black
(Jan. 96-March 96)
[3]-$1,150

C. White Face
(Jan. 95-Jan. 96)
[3]-$465 [2]-$540

A

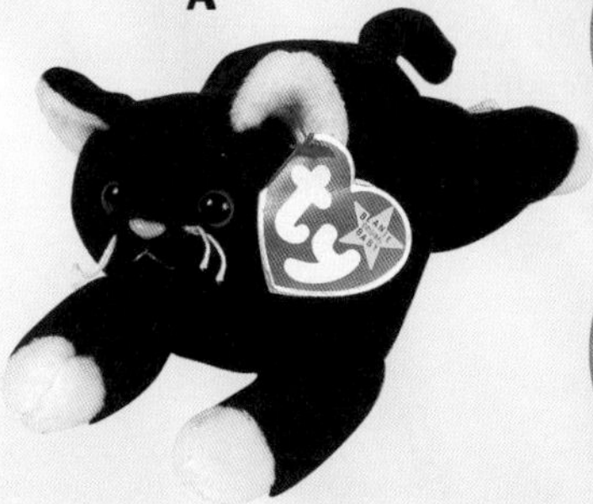

B

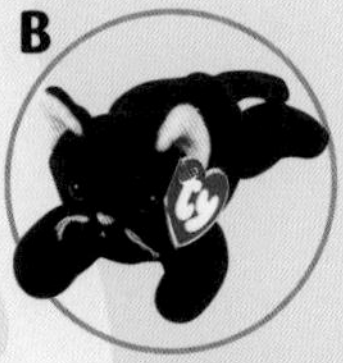

C

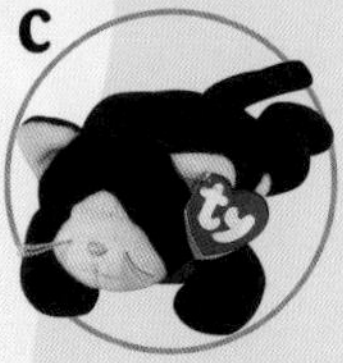

Birthdate: March 28, 1994
Price Paid: $__________
Date Purchased: __________
Tag Generation: __________

Keep Zip by your side all the day through
Zip is good luck, you'll see it's true
When you have something you need to do
Zip will always believe in you!

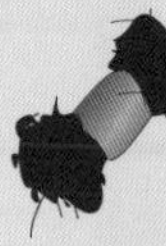

Say Hello To Our New Friends!

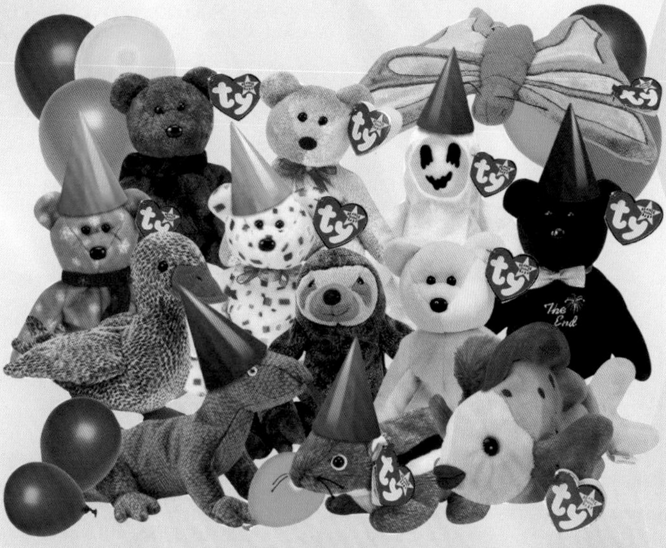

Value Totals: __________

SPORTS PROMOTION BEANIE BABIES®

Sixty-one different *Beanie Babies* have been given away in 94 sporting promotions in the United States and Canada. The most famous, perhaps, is the "Harry Caray 'Daisy'."

SPORTS PROMOTION BEANIE BABIES® KEY

 Canadian Special Olympics

 Major League Baseball

 National Basketball Association

 National Football League

 National Hockey League

 Women's National Basketball Association

1. 1999 Signature Bear™
New York Yankees
5/9/99 · N/A
Market Value: $65

2. Baldy™
Philadelphia 76ers
1/17/98 · LE-5,000
Market Value: $130

3. Baldy™
Washington Capitals
2/20/99 · LE-5,000
Market Value: $70

4. Batty™
Milwaukee Brewers
5/31/98 · LE-12,000
Market Value: $75

5. Batty™
New York Mets
7/12/98 · LE-30,000
Market Value: $85

6. Batty™
Seattle Mariners
5/29/99 · LE-15,000
Market Value: $70

7. Blackie™
Boston Bruins
10/12/98 · LE-5,000
Market Value: $80

8. Blackie™
Chicago Bears
In Club Kits · LE-20,000
Market Value: $70

9. Blackie™
Chicago Bears
11/8/98 · LE-8,000
Market Value: $75

10. Blizzard™
Chicago White Sox
7/12/98 · LE-20,000
Market Value: $85

11. Bones™
Chicago Blackhawks
10/24/98 · LE-5,000
Market Value: $95

12. Bones™
New York Yankees
3/10/98 · N/A
Market Value: $150

13. Bongo™
Charlotte Sting
7/17/98 · LE-3,000
Market Value: $130

14. Bongo™
Cleveland Cavaliers
4/5/98 · LE-5,000
Market Value: $125

15. Chip™
Atlanta Braves
8/19/98 · LE-12,000
Market Value: $80

16. Chocolate™
Dallas Cowboys
9/6/98 · LE-10,000
Market Value: $110

17. Chocolate™
Denver Nuggets
4/17/98 · LE-5,000
Market Value: $110

18. Chocolate™
Seattle Mariners
9/5/98 · LE-10,000
Market Value: $75

19. Chocolate™
Tennessee Oilers
10/18/98 · LE-7,500
Market Value: $75

SPORTS PROMOTION BEANIE BABIES®

	Price Paid	Value of My Collection
1.		
2.		
3.		
4.		
5.		
6.		
7.		
8.		
9.		
10.		
11.		
12.		
13.		
14.		
15.		
16.		
17.		
18.		
19.		

Value Totals: _____

COLLECTOR'S VALUE GUIDE™

VALUE GUIDE – SPORTS PROMOTION BEANIE BABIES®

(20)
Chocolate™
Toronto Maple Leafs
1/2/99 · LE-3,000
Market Value: $100

(21)
Claude™
Sacramento Kings
3/14/99 · LE-5,000
Market Value: $125

(22)
Cubbie™
Chicago Cubs
1/15-1/17/99 · N/A
Market Value: $400

(23)
Cubbie™
Chicago Cubs
1/16-1/18/98 · LE-100
Market Value: $425

(24)
Cubbie™
Chicago Cubs
5/18/97 · LE-10,000
Market Value: $160

(25)
Cubbie™
Chicago Cubs
9/6/97 · LE-10,000
Market Value: $145

(26)
Curly™
Charlotte Sting
6/15/98 · LE-5,000
Market Value: $115

(27)
Curly™
Chicago Bears
12/20/98 · LE-10,000
Market Value: $80

(28)
Curly™
Cleveland Rockers
8/15/98 · LE-3,200
Market Value: $95

(29)
Curly™
New York Mets
8/22/98 · LE-30,000
Market Value: $85

(30)
Curly™
San Antonio Spurs
4/27/98 · LE-2,500
Market Value: $110

(31)
Daisy™
Chicago Cubs
5/3/98 · LE-10,000
Market Value: $330

(32)
Derby™
Houston Astros
8/16/98 · LE-15,000
Market Value: $75

(33)
Derby™
Indianapolis Colts
10/4/98 · LE-10,000
Market Value: $75

(34)
Dotty™
Los Angeles Sparks
7/31/99 · LE-3,000
Market Value: $90

(35)
Early™
Milwaukee Brewers
6/12/99 · LE-12,000
Market Value: $40

(36)
Ears™
Oakland A's
3/15/98 · LE-1,500
Market Value: $160

(37)
Erin™
Chicago Cubs
8/5/99 · LE-12,000
Market Value: N/E

(38)
Fortune™
Kansas City Royals
6/6/99 · LE-10,000
Market Value: $85

(39)
Glory™
All-Star Game
7/7/98 · LE-52,000 approx.
Market Value: $180

(40)
Goatee™
Arizona Diamondbacks
7/8/99 · LE-10,000
Market Value: N/E

(41)
Gobbles™
Phoenix Coyotes
11/26/98 · LE-5,000
Market Value: $70

(42)
Gobbles™
St. Louis Blues
11/24/98 · LE-7,500
Market Value: $70

(43)
Goochy™
Tampa Bay Devil Rays
4/10/99 · LE-10,000
Market Value: $60

(44)
Gracie™
Chicago Cubs
9/13/98 · LE-10,000
Market Value: $120

(45)
Hippie™
Minnesota Twins
6/18/99 · LE-10,000
Market Value: $75

(46)
Hippie™
St. Louis Blues
3/22/99 · LE-7,500
Market Value: $95

SPORTS PROMOTION BEANIE BABIES®		
	Price Paid	Value of My Collection
20.		
21.		
22.		
23.		
24.		
25.		
26.		
27.		
28.		
29.		
30.		
31.		
32.		
33.		
34.		
35.		
36.		
37.		
38.		
39.		
40.		
41.		
42.		
43.		
44.		
45.		
46.		

COLLECTOR'S VALUE GUIDE™

Value Totals: _____

VALUE GUIDE – SPORTS PROMOTION BEANIE BABIES®

(47)
Hissy™
Arizona Diamondbacks
6/14/98 · LE-6,500
Market Value: $80

(48)
KuKu™
Detroit Tigers
7/11/99 · LE-10,000
Market Value: N/E

(49)
Lucky™
Minnesota Twins
7/31/98 · LE-10,000
Market Value: $85

(50)
Luke™
Texas Rangers
9/5/99 · LE-15,000
Market Value: N/E

(51)
Mac™
St. Louis Cardinals
6/14/99 · LE-20,000
Market Value: $60

(52)
Maple™
Canadian Special Olympics
8/97 & 12/97 · N/A
Market Value: $400

(53)
Mel™
Anaheim Angels
9/6/98 · LE-10,000
Market Value: $75

(54)
Mel™
Detroit Shock
7/25/98 · LE-5,000
Market Value: $85

(55)
Millennium™
Chicago Cubs
9/26/99 · LE-40,000
Market Value: N/E

(56)
Millennium™
New York Yankees
8/15/99 · N/A
Market Value: N/E

(57)
Mystic™
Los Angeles Sparks
8/3/98 · LE-5,000
Market Value: $100

(58)
Mystic™
Washington Mystics
7/11/98 · LE-5,000
Market Value: $130

(59)
Peace™
Oakland A's
5/1/99 · LE-10,000
Market Value: $95

(60)
Peanut™
Oakland A's
8/1/98 · LE-15,000
Market Value: $90

(61)
Peanut™
Oakland A's
9/6/98 · LE-15,000
Market Value: $90

(62)
Pinky™
San Antonio Spurs
4/29/98 · LE-2,500
Market Value: $110

(63)
Pinky™
Tampa Bay Devil Rays
8/23/98 · LE-10,000
Market Value: $70

(64)
Pugsly™
Atlanta Braves
9/2/98 · LE-12,000
Market Value: $80

(65)
Pugsly™
Texas Rangers
8/4/98 · LE-10,000
Market Value: $85

(66)
Roam™
Buffalo Sabres
2/19/99 · LE-5,000
Market Value: $80

(67)
Roary™
Kansas City Royals
5/31/98 · LE-13,000
Market Value: $90

(68)
Rocket™
Toronto Blue Jays
9/6/98 · LE-12,000
Market Value: $95

(69)
Rover™
Cincinnati Reds
8/16/98 · LE-15,000
Market Value: $85

(70)
Sammy™
Chicago Cubs
1/15-1/17/99 · N/A
Market Value: $425

(71)
Sammy™
Chicago Cubs
4/25/99 · LE-12,000
Market Value: $90

(72)
Scoop™
Houston Comets
8/6/98 · LE-5,000
Market Value: $95

(73)
Scorch™
Cincinnati Reds
6/19/99 · LE-10,000
Market Value: $75

SPORTS PROMOTION BEANIE BABIES®	Price Paid	Value of My Collection
47.		
48.		
49.		
50.		
51.		
52.		
53.		
54.		
55.		
56.		
57.		
58.		
59.		
60.		
61.		
62.		
63.		
64.		
65.		
66.		
67.		
68.		
69.		
70.		
71.		
72.		
73.		

Value Totals: _____

COLLECTOR'S
VALUE GUIDE™

(74)
Slippery™
San Francisco Giants
4/11/99 · LE-15,000
Market Value: $80

(75)
Sly™
Arizona Diamondbacks
8/27/98 · LE-10,000
Market Value: $85

(76)
Smoochy™
St. Louis Cardinals
8/14/98 · LE-20,000
Market Value: $80

(77)
Snort™
Chicago Bulls
4/10/99 · LE-5,000
Market Value: $70

(78)
Spunky™
Buffalo Sabres
10/23/98 · LE-5,000
Market Value: $80

(79)
Stretch™
New York Yankees
8/9/98 · N/A
Market Value: $75

(80)
Stretch™
St. Louis Cardinals
5/22/98 · LE-20,000
Market Value: $80

(81)
Stripes™
Detroit Tigers
5/31/98 · LE-10,000
Market Value: $90

(82)
Stripes™
Detroit Tigers
8/8/98 · LE-10,000
Market Value: $90

(83)
Strut™
Indiana Pacers
4/2/98 · LE-5,000
Market Value: $85

(84)
Tiny™
Houston Astros
7/18/99 · LE-20,000
Market Value: N/E

(85)
Tuffy™
New Jersey Devils
10/24/98 · LE-5,000
Market Value: $95

(86)
Tuffy™
San Francisco Giants
8/30/98 · LE-10,000
Market Value: $90

(87)
Valentina™
New York Mets
5/30/99 · LE-18,000
Market Value: $85

(88)
Valentino™
Canadian Special Olympics
6/98, 9/98 & 10/98 · N/A
Market Value: $240

(89)
Valentino™
New York Yankees
5/17/98 · LE-10,000
Market Value: $165

(90)
Waddle™
Pittsburgh Penguins
10/24/98 · LE-7,000
Market Value: $90

(91)
Waddle™
Pittsburgh Penguins
11/21/98 · LE-7,000
Market Value: $90

(92)
Waves™
San Diego Padres
8/14/98 · LE-10,000
Market Value: $95

(93)
Weenie™
Tampa Bay Devil Rays
7/26/98 · LE-15,000
Market Value: $85

(94)
Whisper™
Milwaukee Bucks
2/28/99 · LE-5,000
Market Value: $60

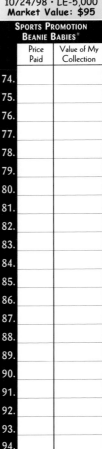

SPORTS PROMOTION BEANIE BABIES®		
	Price Paid	Value of My Collection
74.		
75.		
76.		
77.		
78.		
79.		
80.		
81.		
82.		
83.		
84.		
85.		
86.		
87.		
88.		
89.		
90.		
91.		
92.		
93.		
94.		

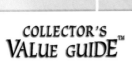
COLLECTOR'S
VALUE GUIDE™

Value Totals: _____

The Beanie Buddies™ Are Getting Bigger!

There have been 45 of the lovable Ty *Beanie Buddies* introduced since 1998. For the Fall of 1999, Ty has released an exciting new assortment of *Buddies*, including two exclusive international bears, two exclusive club bears and "Snowboy," the first *Beanie Buddy* not to have a matching *Beanie Baby*.

1

NEW!

Amber™
Cat · #9341
Issued: August 31, 1999
Current – Just Released
Price Paid: $_____
Market Value: $_____

Beanie Buddies™ Fact
Amber and Silver the Beanie Babies were modeled after two orphaned kittens found by Ty Warner!

2

Beak™
Kiwi · #9301
Issued: September 30, 1998
Retired: March 31, 1999
Price Paid: $_____
Market Value: $45

Beanie Buddies™ Fact
Beak the Beanie Baby and Beak the Beanie Buddy are the first to be released as a set!

3

Bongo™
Monkey · #9312
Issued: January 1, 1999
Current – Easy To Find
Price Paid: $_____
Market Value: $_____

Beanie Buddies™ Fact
Bongo the Beanie Baby was first named Nana. Ty Warner liked the name Bongo better because he plays the Bongos!

Value
Totals: _____

COLLECTOR'S
VALUE GUIDE™

4

NEW!

Britannia™
(exclusive to the United Kingdom)

Bear · #9601
Issued: August 31, 1999
Current – Just Released
Price Paid: $_____
Market Value: $_____

Beanie Buddies™ Fact
Britannia the Beanie Baby was the
first international bear to have an
embroidered flag rather than a patch!

5

Bubbles™

Fish · #9323
Issued: January 1, 1999
Current – Easy To Find
Price Paid: $_____
Market Value: $_____

Beanie Buddies™ Fact
Bubbles the Beanie Baby made
in the swimming position was
quite a challenge to manufacture.

6

Chilly™

Polar Bear · #9317
Issued: January 1, 1999
Current – Moderate To Find
Price Paid: $_____
Market Value: $_____

Beanie Buddies™ Fact
Chilly the Beanie Baby
was introduced in June of 1994 and
retired in January of 1996 making
him one of the most sought after!

7

Chip™

Cat · #9318
Issued: January 1, 1999
Current – Easy To Find
Price Paid: $_____
Market Value: $_____

Beanie Buddies™ Fact
Chip the Beanie Baby due to the
variety of colors and pattern shapes, is
one of the most difficult to produce.
It takes over 20 pieces to make Chip!

COLLECTOR'S
VALUE GUIDE™

Value
Totals: _____

8

NEW!

Clubby™
Bear · #9990
Issued: August 9, 1999
Current – Club Exclusive
Price Paid: $_____
Market Value: $_____

Beanie Buddies™ Fact
Clubby the Beanie Baby was not only
the first BBOC Bear, but also the
first to wear a button!

9

NEW!

Clubby II™
Bear · #9991
Issued: August 9, 1999
Current – Club Exclusive
Price Paid: $_____
Market Value: $_____

Beanie Buddies™ Fact
Clubby II the Beanie Baby was the
first to be included in a BBOC Kit!

10

Erin™
Bear · #9309
Issued: January 1, 1999
Current – Hard To Find
Price Paid: $_____
Market Value: $_____

Beanie Buddies™ Fact
Erin the Beanie Baby is the first
bear to represent a country but not
wear the country's flag!

11

Fetch™
Golden Retriever · #9338
Issued: August 31, 1999
Current – Just Released
Price Paid: $_____
Market Value: $_____

Beanie Buddies™ Fact
Fetch the Beanie Baby was
introduced in May of 1998 and
retired in December of 1998 when
he was less than one year old!

Value
Totals: _____

COLLECTOR'S
VALUE GUIDE™

12

Fuzz™
Bear · #9328
Issued: April 1, 1999
Current – Hard To Find
Price Paid: $_____
Market Value: $_____

Beanie Buddies™ Fact
Fuzz the Beanie Baby is made with
Tylon® that is crimped under
extremely high temperature.

13

NEW!

Gobbles™
Turkey · #9333
Issued: August 31, 1999
Current – Just Released
Price Paid: $_____
Market Value: $_____

Beanie Buddies™ Fact
Gobbles the Beanie Baby had several
different types of waddles, including
single and double felt!

14

NEW!

Halo™
Angel Bear · #9337
Issued: August 31, 1999
Current – Just Released
Price Paid: $_____
Market Value: $_____

Beanie Buddies™ Fact
Halo the Beanie Baby is made from
a special fabric that shimmers.
This fabric makes Halo even
more heavenly!

15

Hippity™
Bunny · #9324
Issued: January 1, 1999
Current – Moderate To Find
Price Paid: $_____
Market Value: $_____

Beanie Buddies™ Fact
Hippity the Beanie Baby is a shade
of green called Spring Mint. Custom
colors like Spring Mint are difficult
to maintain throughout production.

16

Hope™
Bear · #9327
Issued: April 19, 1999
Current – Moderate To Find
Price Paid: $_____
Market Value: $_____

Beanie Buddies™ Fact
The Beanie Baby Hope is the first
Beanie Baby to be modeled after one
of Ty's plush bears!

17

Humphrey™
Camel · #9307
Issued: September 30, 1998
Current – Easy To Find
Price Paid: $_____
Market Value: $_____

Beanie Buddies™ Fact
Humphrey the Beanie Baby
was one of the first to be retired.
Very few were produced,
making him highly collectable!

18

NEW!

Inch™
Inchworm · #9331
Issued: Summer 1999
Current – Very Hard To Find
Price Paid: $_____
Market Value: $_____

Beanie Buddies™ Fact
Inch the Beanie Baby was available
with both felt and yarn antennas!

19

Jabber™
Parrot · #9326
Issued: April 16, 1999
Current – Easy To Find
Price Paid: $_____
Market Value: $_____

Beanie Buddies™ Fact
The Beanie Baby Jabber has 6 colors
of fabric and 17 pattern pieces
which make him not only one of the
most colorful but also one of the
most difficult Beanies to produce!

Value
Totals: _____

COLLECTOR'S
VALUE GUIDE™

20

Jake™
Mallard Duck • #9304
Issued: September 30, 1998
Current – Easy To Find
Price Paid: $_____
Market Value: $_____

Beanie Buddies™ Fact
Jake the Beanie Baby
due to his numerous colors was
difficult to manufacture making him
one of the most sought after!

21

NEW!

Maple™
(exclusive to Canada)
Bear • #9600
Issued: August 31, 1999
Current – Just Released
Price Paid: $_____
Market Value: $_____

Beanie Buddies™ Fact
Maple the Beanie Baby was the first
exclusive international bear!

22

Millennium™
Bear • #9325
Issued: April 9, 1999
Current – Very Hard To Find
Price Paid: $_____
Market Value: $_____

Beanie Buddies™ Fact
The Beanie Baby Millennium
commemorates the new millennium
and therefore is highly collectible!

23

Patti™
Platypus • #9320
Issued: January 1, 1999
Retired: July 27, 1999
Price Paid: $_____
Market Value: $22

Beanie Buddies™ Fact
Patti the Beanie Baby
was one of the original nine.
Patti was available in both
maroon and magenta!

COLLECTOR'S
VALUE GUIDE™

Value Totals: _____

24 NEW!

Peace™
Bear · #9335
Issued: August 31, 1999
Current – Just Released
Price Paid: $_____
Market Value: $_____

Beanie Buddies™ Fact
Peace the Beanie Baby was the first
Beanie Baby with an embroidered
emblem. This Ty-dye technique on a
soft toy is the first in the World!

25

Peanut™
Elephant · #9300
Issued: September 30, 1998
Current – Hard To Find
Price Paid: $_____
Market Value: $_____

Beanie Buddies™ Fact
Peanut the Beanie Baby
made in this royal blue color
is extremely rare and very valuable!

26

Peking™
Panda · #9310
Issued: January 1, 1999
Current – Easy To Find
Price Paid: $_____
Market Value: $_____

Beanie Buddies™ Fact
Peking the Beanie Baby
was the first Panda made by Ty.
He was retired after only six months
making him highly collectible!

27

Pinky™
Flamingo · #9316
Issued: January 1, 1999
Current – Easy To Find
Price Paid: $_____
Market Value: $_____

Beanie Buddies™ Fact
Pinky the Beanie Baby
was a manufacturing challenge
because of her long neck!

Value Totals: _____

COLLECTOR'S
VALUE GUIDE™

28

Princess™
Bear · #9329
Issued: April 23, 1999
Current – Hard To Find
Price Paid: $_____
Market Value: $_____

Beanie Buddies™ Fact
N/A

29

NEW!

Pumkin'™
Pumpkin · #9332
Issued: August 31, 1999
Current – Just Released
Price Paid: $_____
Market Value: $_____

Beanie Buddies™ Fact
Pumkin' the Beanie Baby was the
first Beanie to represent a vegetable!

30

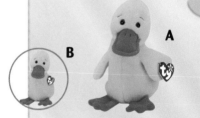

B   A

Quackers™
Duck · #9302
Issued: September 30, 1998
Retired: July 21, 1999
Price Paid: $_____
Market Value:
A. With Wings – $25
B. Without Wings – $240

Beanie Buddies™ Fact
Quackers the Beanie Baby
retired in May 1998,
was once made without wings!

31

Rover™
Dog · #9305
Issued: September 30, 1998
Current – Easy To Find
Price Paid: $_____
Market Value: $_____

Beanie Buddies™ Fact
Rover the Beanie Baby
was the first non-breed dog.
Introduced in the summer of 1996
this red color set him apart!

32

NEW!

Schweetheart™
Orangutan · #9330
Issued: Summer 1999
Current – Very Hard To Find
Price Paid: $_____
Market Value: $_____

Beanie Buddies™ Fact
Schweetheart the Beanie Baby has fabric that is tip dyed. It is made with a special dying process where only the very tips are dyed a separate color. It is a very costly and difficult process!

33

NEW!

Silver™
Cat · #9340
Issued: August 31, 1999
Current – Just Released
Price Paid: $_____
Market Value: $_____

Beanie Buddies™ Fact
Silver and Amber the Beanie Babies were modeled after two orphaned kittens found by Ty Warner!

34

NEW!

Slither™
Snake · #9339
Issued: August 31, 1999
Current – Just Released
Price Paid: $_____
Market Value: $_____

Beanie Buddies™ Fact
Slither the Beanie Baby was the first snake made by Ty. Since his retirement in 1995 he has learned how to coil!

35

Smoochy™
Frog · #9315
Issued: January 1, 1999
Current – Easy To Find
Price Paid: $_____
Market Value: $_____

Beanie Buddies™ Fact
Smoochy the Beanie Baby is the second Beanie Baby frog made by Ty!

Value Totals: _____

COLLECTOR'S
VALUE GUIDE™

36

Snort™
Bull · #9311
Issued: January 1, 1999
Current – Easy To Find
Price Paid: $_____
Market Value: $_____

Beanie Buddies™ Fact
Snort the Beanie Baby
is the second bull made by Ty.
The first bull did not have hooves!

37

NEW!

Snowboy™
Snowboy · #9342
Issued: August 31, 1999
Current – Just Released
Price Paid: $_____
Market Value: $_____

Beanie Buddies™ Fact
Snowboy the Beanie Baby was never
made. This is the first and only time
this pattern will be used!

38

NEW!

Spangle™
Bear · #9336
Issued: August 31, 1999
Current – Just Released
Price Paid: $_____
Market Value: $_____

Beanie Buddies™ Fact
Spangle the Beanie Baby is the
first Beanie to feature two distinct
patterned fabrics and three
different head colors!

39

NEW!

Spinner™
Spider · #9334
Issued: August 31, 1999
Current – Just Released
Price Paid: $_____
Market Value: $_____

Beanie Buddies™ Fact
Spinner the Beanie Baby was the
second spider to be made by Ty. The
attention to detail includes a tiger
striped body and red eyes!

40

Squealer™
Pig · #9313
Issued: January 1, 1999
Current – Easy To Find
Price Paid: $_____
Market Value: $_____

Beanie Buddies™ Fact
Squealer the Beanie Baby
was one of the original nine.
Squealer was so popular that
he didn't retire for over four years!

41

Stretch™
Ostrich · #9303
Issued: September 30, 1998
Current – Easy To Find
Price Paid: $_____
Market Value: $_____

Beanie Buddies™ Fact
Stretch the Beanie Baby
is one of the most difficult to
produce due to her long neck and
numerous parts!

42

Teddy™
Bear · #9306
Issued: September 30, 1998
Current – Hard To Find
Price Paid: $_____
Market Value: $_____

Beanie Buddies™ Fact
Teddy the Beanie Baby
was made in six colors.
A very limited number were produced
in this special cranberry color!

43

Tracker™
Basset Hound · #9319
Issued: January 1, 1999
Current – Easy To Find
Price Paid: $_____
Market Value: $_____

Beanie Buddies™ Fact
Tracker the Beanie Baby
has the most expressive eyes.
Close attention to this detail
means limited production.

**Value
Totals:** _____

COLLECTOR'S
VALUE GUIDE™

44

Twigs™

Giraffe · #9308
Issued: September 30, 1998
Retired: January 1, 1999
Price Paid: $_____
Market Value: $160

Beanie Buddies™ Fact
Twigs the Beanie Baby
was manufactured in fabric
created exclusively for Ty
and was retired in May 1998!

45

Waddle™

Penguin · #9314
Issued: January 1, 1999
Current – Easy To Find
Price Paid: $_____
Market Value: $_____

Beanie Buddies™ Fact
Waddle the Beanie Baby
was the first of two penguins
to be made by Ty.
He was retired in April of 1998!

Say Hello To

Our New Friends!

1

1997 Teenie Beanie Babies™ Complete Set (set/10)
Issued: April 11, 1997
Retired: May 15, 1997
Price Paid: $_____
Market Value: $160

2

1998 Teenie Beanie Babies™ Complete Set (set/12)
Issued: May 22, 1998
Retired: June 12, 1998
Price Paid: $_____
Market Value: $60

3

1999 Teenie Beanie Babies™ Complete Set (set/12)
Issued: May 21, 1999
Retired: June 3, 1999
Price Paid: $_____
Market Value: $45

4

1999 Teenie Beanie Babies™ International Bears (set/4)
Issued: June 4, 1999
Retired: June 17, 1999
Price Paid: $_____
Market Value: $35

5

Antsy™
Anteater
3rd Promotion, #2 of 12
Issued: May 21, 1999
Retired: June 3, 1999
Price Paid: $_____
Market Value: $5

6

Bones™
Dog • 2nd Promotion, #9 of 12
Issued: May 22, 1998
Retired: June 12, 1998
Price Paid: $_____
Market Value: $7

Value Totals: _____

COLLECTOR'S
VALUE GUIDE™

7

Bongo™
Monkey
2nd Promotion, #2 of 12
Issued: May 22, 1998
Retired: June 12, 1998
Price Paid: $_____
Market Value: $14

8

Britannia™
Bear • 4th Promotion
Issued: June 4, 1999
Retired: June 17, 1999
Price Paid: $_____
Market Value: $9

9

Chip™
Cat • 3rd Promotion, #12 of 12
Issued: May 21, 1999
Retired: June 3, 1999
Price Paid: $_____
Market Value: $5

10

Chocolate™
Moose • 1st Promotion, #4 of 10
Issued: April 11, 1997
Retired: May 15, 1997
Price Paid: $_____
Market Value: $28

11

Chops™
Lamb • 1st Promotion, #3 of 10
Issued: April 11, 1997
Retired: May 15, 1997
Price Paid: $_____
Market Value: $30

12

Claude™
Crab • 3rd Promotion, #9 of 12
Issued: May 21, 1999
Retired: June 3, 1999
Price Paid: $_____
Market Value: $5

**COLLECTOR'S
VALUE GUIDE™**

Value
Totals: _____

13

Doby™
Doberman
2nd Promotion, #1 of 12
Issued: May 22, 1998
Retired: June 12, 1998
Price Paid: $_____
Market Value: $14

14

Erin™
Bear • 4th Promotion
Issued: June 4, 1999
Retired: June 17, 1999
Price Paid: $_____
Market Value: $9

15

Freckles™
Leopard
3rd Promotion, #1 of 12
Issued: May 21, 1999
Retired: June 3, 1999
Price Paid: $_____
Market Value: $5

16

Glory™
Bear • 4th Promotion
Issued: June 4, 1999
Retired: June 17, 1999
Price Paid: $_____
Market Value:
A. Glory™ – $9
B. McDonald's Employee
Bear – $24

17

Goldie™
Goldfish
1st Promotion, #5 of 10
Issued: April 11, 1997
Retired: May 15, 1997
Price Paid: $_____
Market Value: $22

18

Happy™
Hippo • 2nd Promotion, #6 of 12
Issued: May 22, 1998
Retired: June 12, 1998
Price Paid: $_____
Market Value: $6

**Value
Totals: _____**

COLLECTOR'S
VALUE GUIDE™

19

Iggy™
Iguana
3rd Promotion, #6 of 12
Issued: May 21, 1999
Retired: June 3, 1999
Price Paid: $_____
Market Value: $5

20

Inch™
Inchworm
2nd Promotion, #4 of 12
Issued: May 22, 1998
Retired: June 12, 1998
Price Paid: $_____
Market Value: $6

21

Lizz™
Lizard
1st Promotion, #10 of 10
Issued: April 11, 1997
Retired: May 15, 1997
Price Paid: $_____
Market Value: $17

22

Maple™
Bear · 4th Promotion
Issued: June 4, 1999
Retired: June 17, 1999
Price Paid: $_____
Market Value: $9

23

Mel™
Koala · 2nd Promotion, #7 of 12
Issued: May 22, 1998
Retired: June 12, 1998
Price Paid: $_____
Market Value: $6

24

'Nook™
Husky
3rd Promotion, #11 of 12
Issued: May 21, 1999
Retired: June 3, 1999
Price Paid: $_____
Market Value: $5

COLLECTOR'S
VALUE GUIDE™

Value
Totals: _____

25

Nuts™
Squirrel
3rd Promotion, #8 of 12
Issued: May 21, 1999
Retired: June 3, 1999
Price Paid: $_____
Market Value: $5

26

Patti™
Platypus
1st Promotion, #1 of 10
Issued: April 11, 1997
Retired: May 15, 1997
Price Paid: $_____
Market Value: $32

27

Peanut™
Elephant
2nd Promotion, #12 of 12
Issued: May 22, 1998
Retired: June 12, 1998
Price Paid: $_____
Market Value: $7

28

Pinchers™
Lobster
2nd Promotion, #5 of 12
Issued: May 22, 1998
Retired: June 12, 1998
Price Paid: $_____
Market Value: $6

29

Pinky™
Flamingo
1st Promotion, #2 of 10
Issued: April 11, 1997
Retired: May 15, 1997
Price Paid: $_____
Market Value: $42

30

Quacks™
Duck · 1st Promotion, #9 of 10
Issued: April 11, 1997
Retired: May 15, 1997
Price Paid: $_____
Market Value: $16

Value Totals: _____

COLLECTOR'S
VALUE GUIDE™

31

Rocket™
Blue Jay
3rd Promotion, #5 of 12
Issued: May 21, 1999
Retired: June 3, 1999
Price Paid: $_____
Market Value: $5

32

Scoop™
Pelican
2nd Promotion, #8 of 12
Issued: May 22, 1998
Retired: June 12, 1998
Price Paid: $_____
Market Value: $7

33

Seamore™
Seal · 1st Promotion, #7 of 10
Issued: April 11, 1997
Retired: May 15, 1997
Price Paid: $_____
Market Value: $22

34

Smoochy™
Frog · 3rd Promotion, #3 of 12
Issued: May 21, 1999
Retired: June 3, 1999
Price Paid: $_____
Market Value: $5

35

Snort™
Bull · 1st Promotion, #8 of 10
Issued: April 11, 1997
Retired: May 15, 1997
Price Paid: $_____
Market Value: $15

36

Speedy™
Turtle · 1st Promotion, #6 of 10
Issued: April 11, 1997
Retired: May 15, 1997
Price Paid: $_____
Market Value: $22

COLLECTOR'S
VALUE GUIDE™

Value
Totals: _____

37

Spunky™
Cocker Spaniel
3rd Promotion, #4 of 12
Issued: May 21, 1999
Retired: June 3, 1999
Price Paid: $_____
Market Value: $5

38

Stretchy™
Ostrich
3rd Promotion, #10 of 12
Issued: May 21, 1999
Retired: June 3, 1999
Price Paid: $_____
Market Value: $5

39

Strut™
Rooster
3rd Promotion, #7 of 12
Issued: May 21, 1999
Retired: June 3, 1999
Price Paid: $_____
Market Value: $5

40

Twigs™
Giraffe
2nd Promotion, #3 of 12
Issued: May 22, 1998
Retired: June 12, 1998
Price Paid: $_____
Market Value: $14

41

Waddle™
Penguin
2nd Promotion, #11 of 12
Issued: May 22, 1998
Retired: June 12, 1998
Price Paid: $_____
Market Value: $7

42

Zip™
Cat · 2nd Promotion, #10 of 12
Issued: May 22, 1998
Retired: June 12, 1998
Price Paid: $_____
Market Value: $8

Value Totals: _____

COLLECTOR'S
VALUE GUIDE™

TOTAL VALUE OF MY COLLECTION

BEANIE BABIES® VALUE TOTALS	BEANIE BABIES® VALUE TOTALS	BEANIE BABIES® VALUE TOTALS
Page 27	Page 52	Page 77
Page 28	Page 53	Page 78
Page 29	Page 54	Page 79
Page 30	Page 55	Page 80
Page 31	Page 56	Page 81
Page 32	Page 57	Page 82
Page 33	Page 58	Page 83
Page 34	Page 59	Page 84
Page 35	Page 60	Page 85
Page 36	Page 61	Page 86
Page 37	Page 62	Page 87
Page 38	Page 63	Page 88
Page 39	Page 64	Page 89
Page 40	Page 65	Page 90
Page 41	Page 66	Page 91
Page 42	Page 67	Page 92
Page 43	Page 68	Page 93
Page 44	Page 69	Page 94
Page 45	Page 70	Page 95
Page 46	Page 71	Page 96
Page 47	Page 72	Page 97
Page 48	Page 73	Page 98
Page 49	Page 74	Page 99
Page 50	Page 75	Page 100
Page 51	Page 76	Page 101
Subtotal	Subtotal	Subtotal

COLLECTOR'S VALUE GUIDE™

Page Total: _____

TOTAL VALUE OF MY COLLECTION

BEANIE BABIES®
VALUE TOTALS

Page 102 _____

Page 103 _____

Page 104 _____

Page 105 _____

Page 106 _____

Page 107 _____

Page 108 _____

Page 109 _____

Page 110 _____

Page 111 _____

Page 112 _____

Page 113 _____

Page 114 _____

Page 115 _____

Page 116 _____

Page 117 _____

Page 118 _____

Page 119 _____

Page 120 _____

Page 121 _____

Page 122 _____

Page 123 _____

Page 124 _____

Subtotal _____

BEANIE BABIES®
VALUE TOTALS

Page 125 _____

Page 126 _____

Page 127 _____

Page 128 _____

Page 129 _____

Page 130 _____

Page 131 _____

Page 132 _____

Page 133 _____

Page 134 _____

Page 135 _____

Page 136 _____

Page 137 _____

Subtotal _____

SPORTS PROMOTION BEANIE BABIES®
VALUE TOTALS

Page 138 _____

Page 139 _____

Page 140 _____

Page 141 _____

Subtotal _____

BEANIE BUDDIES™
VALUE TOTALS

Page 142 _____

Page 143 _____

Page 144 _____

Page 145 _____

Page 146 _____

Page 147 _____

Page 148 _____

Page 149 _____

Page 150 _____

Page 151 _____

Page 152 _____

Page 153 _____

Subtotal _____

TEENIE BEANIE BABIES™
VALUE TOTALS

Page 154 _____

Page 155 _____

Page 156 _____

Page 157 _____

Page 158 _____

Page 159 _____

Page 160 _____

Subtotal _____

Grand Total: _____

COLLECTOR'S VALUE GUIDE™

SHOPPING THE SECONDARY MARKET

On August 31, Ty announced that all Ty *Beanies* are scheduled to retire December 31, 1999. So after this date, where can one go to find these cuddly stuffed critters? The answer is the secondary market.

The secondary market serves as a liaison between collectors who are looking to buy, sell or trade pieces that are no longer available in stores. You will find many retired or hard-to-find pieces that are not available at retail prices. Even exclusive pieces, such as the very limited "#1 Bear," given to Ty sales representatives, can be found using this invaluable resource.

HOW DO I GET THERE?

There are several ways to access the secondary market. One of the easiest and most popular ways is to use the Internet. Once on-line, you will find a wide variety of ways to reach other collectors and dealers who are interested in selling pieces or purchasing from your collection. Auction sites and bulletin boards are good starting points in your search for elusive pieces.

Another way to find the *Beanie Babies* you need is to check your local newspaper. *Beanie Babies* are often listed in the classified section under "Collectibles," while many newspapers list *Beanie Babies* as their own separate category. Attending swap and sells can be a fun way to meet local collectors and view their collections while you expand your own.

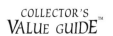

ESTIMATING VALUE

There are several items that may affect the value of your *Beanie Baby*. Availability is a big factor. *Beanie Babies* that were produced in a limited quantity, or were only available in retail stores for a short period of time, are more likely to

capture higher prices on the secondary market than other pieces. *Beanie Babies* that have variations – such as changes in fabric or design changes – also tend to fetch higher prices on the secondary market. The tag generation is another factor that can affect the value of your piece. For instance, a "Legs" the frog with a first generation swing tag is worth $440, while the same piece with a fourth generation swing tag is worth $23, even though the piece looks exactly the same. The older generation tags usually command a higher value on the secondary market. See the *Ty® Swing Tags And Tush Tags* section on the next page for a more detailed explanation.

CARING FOR YOUR COLLECTION

If you are looking to resell your pieces, make sure that you keep them in mint or "as good as new" condition. These are the collectibles that fetch the higher prices. Thinning or

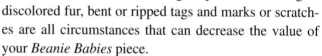

discolored fur, bent or ripped tags and marks or scratches are all circumstances that can decrease the value of your *Beanie Babies* piece.

In order to keep your *Beanie Baby* looking its best, follow some general rules. Keep your *Beanie Babies* in a place where they will not be stepped on, spilled on or mangled by the family pet. You may store your pieces in plastic containers to prevent them from being damaged. Since the swing tag is an important factor in determining a piece's secondary market value, tag protectors are also sold to prevent the animal's swing tag from being ripped or torn.

TY® SWING TAGS AND TUSH TAGS

Any serious *Beanie Baby* collector should know the importance of the animals' tags. Although the tags carry warnings for the consumer to remove them, doing so could reduce the collectible's secondary market value.

Ty's products come with two kinds of tags: a swing tag and a tush tag. The swing tag is the heart-shaped paper tag that is affixed to the animal with a plastic attachment. The tush tag is a small cloth tag near the animal's posterior.

Because both tags are important in estimating the value of an animal, they should be kept in mint condition. By identifying the swing tag generation, collectors can determine the time frame in which the piece was produced. Pieces with older tags usually fetch higher prices on the secondary market than their more recent versions.

Beanie Babies® Swing Tags

Generation 1 (Early 1994-Mid 1994): These single sheet tags feature a red heart with "ty" printed on the front in skinny lettering. The animal's name, style number, reference to "The Beanie Babies Collection" and company information all appear on the back.

> The Beanie Babies Collection
> Brownie ™ style 4010
> © 1993 Ty Inc. Oakbrook, IL. USA
> All Rights Reserved. Caution:
> Remove this tag before giving
> toy to a child. For ages 5 and up.
> Handmade in Korea.
> Surface
> Wash.

Generation 2 (Mid 1994-Early 1995): While the outside is identical to the first generation tag, this tag opens like a book. The inside of this tag contains the animal's name and style number, a "to/from/with love" section for gift giving, a reference to "The Beanie Babies Collection," plus care, cautionary and company information.

> The Beanie Babies Collection
> © 1993 Ty Inc. Oakbrook, IL. USA
> All Rights Reserved, Caution:
> Remove this tag before giving
> toy to a child. For ages 3 and up.
> Handmade in China
> Surface
> Wash.

> Chilly ™ style 4012
> to _____
> from _____
> with love

Ty® Swing Tags And Tush Tags

Generation 3 (Early 1995-Early 1996): Unlike previous tags, the "ty" logo on this generation tag is puffy. The information on the inside of the tag is the same, with the addition of a trademark symbol and Ty Inc.'s three corporate addresses.

The Beanie Babies ™ Collection

Garcia ™ style 4051

© Ty Inc.
Oakbrook IL. U.S.A.
© Ty UK Ltd.
Waterlooville, Hants
PO8 8HH
© Ty Deutschland
90008 Nürnberg
Handmade in China

to _____
from _____
with
love

Generation 4 (Early 1996-Late 1997): A yellow star containing the words "Original Beanie Baby" was added to the front of this tag. The inside underwent major format changes as a poem and a birthdate were added for each animal, and the Ty web site address was included.

The Beanie Babies™Collection

Doodle™ style 4171

© Ty Inc.
Oakbrook IL. U.S.A.
© Ty UK Ltd.
Fareham, Hants
PO15 5TX
© Ty Deutschland
90008 Nürnberg
Handmade in China

DATE OF BIRTH : 3 - 8 - 96
Listen closely to "cock-a-doodle-doo!"
What's the rooster saying to you?
Hurry, wake up sleepy head
We have lots to do, get out of bed!
Visit our web page!!!
http://www.ty.com

Generation 5 (Late 1997-Current): While the only change on the outside of this tag is the typeface of the phrase "Original Beanie Baby," the inside is quite different. The birthday is written out, and "http://" is removed from the Internet address. The piece's style number is deleted (it can be found in the last four digits of the UPC code on the back) and the corporate offices of Ty U.K. and Ty Deutschland are consolidated as Ty Europe Ltd. in Fareham, Hants. Also, the name "Beanie Babies Collection" became registered (®).

The Beanie Babies Collection®

Pinky™

© Ty Inc.
Oakbrook, IL. U.S.A.
© Ty Europe Ltd.
Fareham, Hants
PO15 5TX, U.K.
© Ty Canada
Aurora, Ontario
Handmade in China

DATE OF BIRTH: February 13, 1995
Pinky loves the everglades
From the hottest pink she's made
With floppy legs and big orange beak
She's the Beanie that you seek !
www.ty.com

In the summer of 1998, some 5th generation tags began appearing with subtle differences. The writing in the star logo has a different font, making the word "Original" appear smaller and the letters in the word "Baby" closer together. The font on the inside of the tag is larger and darker, as is the writing on the back of the tag. And in January 1999, the Ty Europe Ltd. address was changed to Gosport, Hampshire, U.K.

The Beanie Babies Collection®

© Ty Inc.
Oakbrook, IL. U.S.A.
© Ty Europe
Gosport, Hampshire, U.K.
© Ty Canada
Aurora, Ontario
Handmade in China

Beanie Babies® Tush Tags

Version 1: The first *Beanie Babies* tush tags are white with black printing and they list company and production information.

© 1993 TY INC., OAKBROOK IL, U.S.A. ALL RIGHTS RESERVED HAND MADE IN CHINA SURFACE WASHABLE

ALL NEW MATERIAL POLYESTER FIBER & P.V.C. PELLETS PA. REG #1965 FOR AGES 3 AND UP

Version 2: The red heart Ty logo is added and the information on the tush tag is printed in red.

Version 3: This tag features the addition of the name of the animal below the Ty heart and "The *Beanie Babies* Collection™" above the heart.

The Beanie Babies Collection™

Quackers

HAND MADE IN CHINA
© 1995 TY INC.
OAKBROOK IL, U.S.A.
SURFACE WASHABLE
ALL NEW MATERIAL
POLYESTER FIBER
& P.V.C. PELLETS
REG. NO PA. 1965(KR)

HAND MADE IN CHINA
© 1993 TY INC.,
OAKBROOK IL, U.S.A.
SURFACE WASHABLE
ALL NEW MATERIAL
POLYESTER FIBER &
P.V.C. PELLETS
REG. NO PA - 1965(KR)
FOR AGES 3 AND UP

Version 4: This tush tag sports a small red star on the upper left-hand side of the Ty heart logo. On some tags, a clear sticker with the star was placed next to the Ty logo.

The Beanie Babies Collection™

Tuffy

HAND MADE IN CHINA
© 1996 TY INC.,
OAKBROOK IL, U.S.A.
SURFACE WASHABLE
ALL NEW MATERIAL
POLYESTER FIBER
& P.V.C. PELLETS
REG. NO PA. 1965(KR)

Version 5: In late 1997, these tags began to appear with a registration mark (®) after "Beanie Babies" in the collection's name and a trademark (™) after the animal's name.

The Beanie Babies® Collection™

Hissy™

HAND MADE IN CHINA
© 1997 TY INC,
OAKBROOK IL, U.S.A.
SURFACE WASHABLE
ALL NEW MATERIAL
POLYESTER FIBER
& P.V.C. PELLETS
REG. NO PA. 1965(KR)

Version 6: These tags feature another slight change in trademark symbols. The registration mark in the collection's name moved from after "Beanie Babies" to after "Collection." Some of the recent *Beanie Baby* tush tags have also noted a change to "P.E." pellets from "P.V.C."

The Beanie Babies® Collection®

Fetch™

HAND MADE IN CHINA
© 1998 TY INC.,
OAKBROOK IL, U.S.A.
SURFACE WASHABLE
ALL NEW MATERIAL
POLYESTER FIBER
& P.E. PELLETS
REG. NO PA. 1965(KR)

Also, in mid-1998, a red stamp began to appear inside some *Beanie Babies'* tush tags. The stamp is an oval containing numbers and Chinese writing.

Millenium™

HANDMADE IN CHINA
© 1999 TY INC.,
OAKBROOK, IL. U.S.A.
SURFACE WASHABLE
ALL NEW MATERIAL
POLYESTER FIBER
& P.E. PELLETS
REG. NO PA. 1965(KR)

Version 7: This version features a hologram on the tush tag, as well as a red heart printed in disappearing ink.

Version 8: In the summer of 1999, the hologrammed tush tags began to appear as a single flap, rather than the looped tag which had been used previously.

PHOTO UNAVAILABLE

Beanie Buddies™ Swing Tags

Generation 1: So far, there is only one generation swing tag for the *Beanie Buddies*. It's the same size as the *Beanie Babies* tags and, on the outside, looks like a *Beanie Baby* generation 5 swing tag (except the word "Buddy" is inside the yellow star instead of the word "Baby"). The inside of the tag has the name of the animal and a fact about its *Beanie Baby* counterpart. After the initial release in which the tags gave the Ty Europe Ltd. address as Fareham, Hants, the tag was changed to read "Gasport, Hampshire, U.K." This was later changed to the correct name of Gosport, Hampshire, U.K.

The Beanie Buddies Collection®
© Ty Inc.
Oakbrook, IL. U.S.A.
© Ty Europe Ltd.
Fareham, Hants
PO15 5TX, U.K.
© Ty Canada
Aurora, Ontario
Handmade in China

Rover ™
Rover the BEANIE BABY was the first non-breed dog. Introduced in the summer of 1996 this red color set him apart!
www.ty.com

The Beanie Buddies Collection®
© Ty Inc.
Oakbrook, IL. U.S.A.
© Ty Europe
Gosport, Hampshire, U.K.
© Ty Canada
Aurora, Ontario
Handmade in China

The Beanie Buddies Collection®
© Ty Inc.
Oakbrook, IL. U.S.A.
© Ty Europe
Gosport, Hampshire, U.K.
© Ty Canada
Aurora, Ontario
Handmade in China

Beanie Buddies™ Tush Tags

Version 1: The first *Beanie Buddies* tush tag is white with a red heart containing the word "ty" in white letters. The back of the tag gives the company name and fabric information in black ink.

TY, INC. ©1998
OAKBROOK, IL.—
REG.NO.PA-1965(KR)
ALL NEW MATERIAL
CONTENTS.POLYESTER
FIBER & P.E. PELLETS
IN CLOTH BAG
HAND MADE IN CHINA
CE

The Beanie Buddies Collection ®
Ty Inc ©1998
OAKBROOK, IL.,
REG.NO.PA-1965(KR)
CONTENTS:POLYESTER
FIBER & P.E.PELLETS
HAND MADE IN CHINA
CE

Version 2: The second *Buddies* tush tags include "The Beanie Buddies Collection®" above the heart. On the back of the tags are the company name and fabric information. All printing is in red ink.

The Beanie Buddies Collection ®
SHELL 100% TYLON ®
Ty Inc ©1999
OAKBROOK, IL.,
REG.NO.PA-1965(KR)
ALL NEW MATERIAL
INNER CONTENTS:
POLYESTER FIBER
& P.E. PELLETS
IN CLOTH BAG
HAND MADE IN CHINA
CE

Version 3: The most recent *Beanie Buddy* tush tags say "Shell 100% Tylon" on the front, and "Inner Contents" on the back.

Teenie Beanie Babies™ Swing Tags

1997 Version: These tags are the single, non-folded type with the red, gold and white front design featuring the "ty" logo with puffy lettering. On the tag's back, the name of the collection and the animal's name (both with the trademark symbols "TM/MC") are printed, as well as company information.

1998 Version: The front of the 1998 tag is the same; however, the back of the tag now sports the official Ty web site address and a change in typeface. Additionally, the trademark symbols now read "TM/MC/MR." Slight spacing differences are also apparent due to multiple production sources.

1999 Version: These swing tags are larger and fatter than the previous tags. The "ty" logo on the front of the tag is no longer embossed in gold, and a yellow star with the words "Original Teenie Beanie" has been added to the front of the tag. The font on the back of the tag has been changed again, and the animal type has been added after its name. The trademark symbol now reads only "™."

Teenie Beanie Babies™ Tush Tags

The tush tags on the *Teenie Beanie Babies* feature the red "ty" heart logo, company and production information and date of copyright printed in red ink. The 1999 tags have a larger, fatter "ty" logo.

The reverse sides of the tags are printed in black ink and contain content information and the name of the manufacturing company – either Simon Marketing of Los Angeles or M-B Sales of Westmont, Illinois. There are also small differences regarding content information and McDonald's corporate name.

VARIATION NEWS

One of the most exciting aspects of collecting *Beanie Babies* is trying to find unique qualities or differences between your *Beanies* and others of the same name. Variations are not only fun to find – sometimes they can reap monetary rewards as well. While many variations do not affect a piece's secondary market value, some rare or unusual variations may cause a piece's value to skyrocket.

COLOR CHANGES

"Spangle" arrived in retail stores with three different colored heads: red, white and blue. Other *Beanie Babies* who have undergone color changes include "Batty," who was available in both brown and tie-dyed fabrics; "Digger," who changed from orange to red; "Happy," who went from feeling gray to a perky pink; and, of course, "Peanut," whose earlier dark blue version is one of the most valuable *Beanie Babies* on the secondary market today.

DESIGN CHANGES

Some *Beanie Babies* underwent design changes, such as "Derby" and "Mystic," who both had their manes changed from fine hair to coarse hair to fluffy hair. "Derby" later added a star to his forehead, while "Mystic's" horn turned iridescent. All of the "Teddy" bears can be found with two face styles, while "Princess" can be found stuffed with P.E. or P.V.C. pellets.

Following the lead of his *Beanie Baby* counterpart, "Quackers" the *Beanie Buddy* began to show up at retail stores without his wings after his recent July retirement. Maybe his lack of wings explains why it took so long for this variation to arrive in stores!

COLLECTOR'S
VALUE GUIDE™

NAME CHANGES

A number of *Beanie Babies* were renamed during the course of their production. Examples of this include "Brownie/Cubbie," "Doodle/Strut" and "Nana/Bongo." Oftentimes, *Beanie Babies'* names were either incorrectly spelled on their tags or the *Beanies* were shipped with a completely wrong tag; however, "Creepy/Spinner" and "Pride/Maple" were produced with the wrong names on the tags. Shortly after production, these mistakes were discovered and fixed, so there are a very limited amount of these variations available.

The
Beanie Babies
Collection®
★ ty®
Creepy™
HAND MADE IN CHINA
© 1996 TY INC.
OAKBROOK IL, U.S.A.
SURFACE WASHABLE
ALL NEW MATERIAL
POLYESTER FIBER
& P.V.C. PELLETS CE
REG. NO. PA. 1965(KR)

The
Beanie Babies
Collection®
★ ty®
Spinner™
HAND MADE IN CHINA
© 1996 TY INC.
OAKBROOK IL, U.S.A.
SURFACE WASHABLE
ALL NEW MATERIAL
POLYESTER FIBER
& P.V.C. PELLETS CE
REG. NO. PA. 1965(KR)

OTHER VARIATIONS

In addition to the changes that are planned by Ty Inc., there are always a number of unintentional errors that make their way into the marketplace as well. One of the most common variation of this kind is a misspelling on a swing or tush tag, such as "Millenium" ("Millennium"), "Spook" ("Spooky") and "Tuck" ("Tusk"). Another common error is upside down or missing flags on the *Beanie Babies*. "Lefty" the donkey, "Righty" the elephant and, more recently, "Osito" the bear are among the animals who have been spotted wearing upside down flags.

Millenium™
DATE OF BIRTH: January 1, 1999
A brand new century has come to call
Health and happiness to one and all
Bring on the fireworks and all the fun
Let's keep the party going 'til 2001 !
www.ty.com

Millennium™
DATE OF BIRTH: January 1, 1999
A brand new century has come to call
Health and happiness to one and all
Bring on the fireworks and all the fun
Let's keep the party going 'til 2001 !
www.ty.com

COUNTERFEIT ALERT!

There are two kinds of *Beanie Babies* on the collectible market: genuine ones and fake ones. Whether you're an avid collector or someone who only has a few of the stuffed toys, it's important to know the differences between genuine and fake ones to protect yourself from purchasing an imposter.

Authentic

CHECK THE TAGS

Perhaps the easiest way to spot a counterfeit is by inspecting its tags. Swing tags should not have smeared ink, jagged edges, uneven gold foil around the front of the heart or errors in spelling and punctuation. The generation of the swing tag should be correct. (See page 165 for tag information.) Also, fake tush tags may be wider than the genuine ones, and the ink may be smeared or blurry.

Counterfeit

INSPECT THE STITCHING

Authentic

Another way to spot a *Beanie* imposter is by seeing how it's made. Genuine *Beanie Babies* are intentionally under-stuffed, so an overstuffed animal or a drastic reduction or absence of pellets should send up caution flags. Fake *Beanie Babies* may have colors that bleed or look dyed, messy stitching, uneven seams or fur that is too shiny or dull. Also, many counterfeits have wrong ribbons and noses that are the wrong colors.

BE A SMART SHOPPER

Counterfeit

Know what genuine *Beanie Babies* look like before purchasing on the secondary market, especially if you do not know the seller. And take your genuine *Beanie Babies* with you to swap and sells to use as comparisons. These precautions can help protect your investment, especially if you try to resell.

COLLECTOR'S
VALUE GUIDE™

BEANIE BABIES® BIRTHDAYS

New releases are listed in pink

Jan. 1, 1999 - **Millennium**™
Jan. 1, 2000 - **Ty 2K**™
Jan. 2, 1998 - **Zero**™
Jan. 3, 1993 - **Spot**™
Jan. 5, 1997 - **KuKu**™
Jan. 6, 1993 - **Patti**™
Jan. 8, 1999 - **Tiptoe**™
Jan. 10, 1999 - **Groovy**™
Jan. 13, 1996 - **Crunch**™

Jan. 14, 1997 - **Spunky**™
Jan. 15, 1996 - **Mel**™
Jan. 17, 1998 - **Slippery**™
Jan. 18, 1994 - **Bones**™
Jan. 21, 1996 - **Nuts**™
Jan. 23, 1999 - **Schweetheart**™
Jan. 25, 1995 - **Peanut**™
Jan. 26, 1996 - **Chip**™
Jan. 25, 1999 - **Wallace**™

Feb. 1, 1996 - **Peace**™
Feb. 3, 1998 - **Beak**™
Feb. 4, 1997 - **Fetch**™
Feb. 5, 1999 - **Osito**™
Feb. 9, 1999 - **Scaly**™
Feb. 11, 1999 - **Silver**™
Feb. 13, 1995 - **Pinky**™
Feb. 13, 1995 - **Stinky**™
Feb. 14, 1994 - **Valentino**™
Feb. 14, 1998 - **Valentina**™

Feb. 17, 1996 - **Baldy**™
Feb. 19, 1998 - **Prickles**™
Feb. 20, 1996 - **Roary**™
Feb. 21, 1999 - **Amber**™
Feb. 22, 1995 - **Tank**™
Feb. 23, 1999 - **Paul**™
Feb. 25, 1994 - **Happy**™
Feb. 27, 1996 - **Sparky**™
Feb. 28, 1995 - **Flip**™

Mar. 1, 1998 - **Ewey**™
Mar. 2, 1995 - **Coral**™
Mar. 6, 1994 - **Nip**™
Mar. 8, 1996 - **Doodle**™
Mar. 8, 1996 - **Strut**™
Mar. 9, 1999 - **Clubby II**™
Mar. 10, 1999 - **Swirly**™
Mar. 11, 1999 - **Honks**™
Mar. 12, 1997 - **Rocket**™
Mar. 14, 1994 - **Ally**™

Mar. 15, 1999 - **Lips**™
Mar. 17, 1997 - **Erin**™
Mar. 19, 1996 - **Seaweed**™
Mar. 20, 1997 - **Early**™
Mar. 21, 1996 - **Fleece**™
Mar. 23, 1998 - **Hope**™
Mar. 25, 1999 - **Knuckles**™
Mar. 28, 1994 - **Zip**™
Mar. 29, 1998 - **Loosy**™

BEANIE BABIES® BIRTHDAYS

April 1, 1999 - **Neon**™
April 3, 1996 - **Hoppity**™
April 4, 1997 - **Hissy**™
April 5, 1997 - **Whisper**™
April 6, 1998 - **Nibbler**™
April 7, 1997 - **Gigi**™
April 10, 1998 - **Eggbert**™
April 12, 1996 - **Curly**™
April 14, 1999 - **Almond**™

April 15, 1999 - **Pecan**™
April 16, 1997 - **Jake**™
April 18, 1995 - **Ears**™
April 19, 1994 - **Quackers**™
April 21, 1999 - **Chipper**™
April 23, 1993 - **Squealer**™
April 25, 1993 - **Legs**™
April 27, 1993 - **Chocolate**™
April 28, 1999 - **Eucalyptus**™

May 1, 1995 - **Lucky**™
May 1, 1996 - **Wrinkles**™
May 2, 1996 - **Pugsly**™
May 3, 1996 - **Chops**™
May 4, 1998 - **Hippie**™
May 7, 1998 - **Nibbly**™
May 10, 1994 - **Daisy**™
May 11, 1995 - **Lizzy**™

May 13, 1993 - **Flash**™
May 15, 1995 - **Snort**™
May 15, 1995 - **Tabasco**™
May 18, 1999 - **Cheeks**™
May 19, 1995 - **Twigs**™
May 20, 1999 - **Slowpoke**™
May 21, 1994 - **Mystic**™
May 27, 1998 - **Scat**™
May 28, 1996 - **Floppity**™
May 29, 1998 - **Canyon**™
May 30, 1996 - **Rover**™
May 31, 1997 - **Wise**™

June 1, 1996 - **Hippity**™
June 2, 1999 - **Flitter**™
June 3, 1996 - **Freckles**™
June 3, 1996 - **Scottie**™
June 4, 1999 - **Wiser**™
June 5, 1997 - **Tracker**™
June 8, 1995 - **Bucky**™
June 8, 1995 - **Manny**™
June 10, 1998 - **Mac**™

June 11, 1995 - **Stripes**™
June 14, 1999 - **Spangle**™
June 15, 1996 - **Scottie**™
June 15, 1998 - **Luke**™
June 16, 1998 - **Stilts**™
June 17, 1996 - **Gracie**™
June 19, 1993 - **Pinchers**™
June 23, 1998 - **Sammy**™
June 27, 1995 - **Bessie**™

July

July 1, 1996 - **Maple™**
July 1, 1996 - **Scoop™**
July 2, 1995 - **Bubbles™**
July 4, 1996 - **Lefty™**
July 4, 1996 - **Righty™**
July 4, 1997 - **Glory™**

July 7, 1998 - **Clubby™**
July 8, 1993 - **Splash™**
July 14, 1995 - **Ringo™**
July 15, 1994 - **Blackie™**
July 19, 1995 - **Grunt™**
July 20, 1995 - **Weenie™**
July 23, 1998 - **Fuzz™**
July 28, 1996 - **Freckles™**
July 31, 1998 - **Scorch™**

August

Aug. 1, 1995 - **Garcia™**
Aug. 1, 1998 - **Mooch™**
Aug. 9, 1995 - **Hoot™**
Aug. 12, 1997 - **Iggy™**
Aug. 13, 1996 - **Spike™**
Aug. 14, 1994 - **Speedy™**
Aug. 16, 1998 - **Kicks™**

Aug. 17, 1995 - **Bongo™**
Aug. 23, 1995 - **Digger™**
Aug. 27, 1995 - **Sting™**
Aug. 28, 1997 - **Pounce™**
Aug. 31, 1998 - **Halo™**

September

Sept. 3, 1995 - **Inch™**
Sept. 3, 1996 - **Claude™**
Sept. 5, 1995 - **Magic™**
Sept. 8, 1998 - **Tiny™**
Sept. 9, 1997 - **Bruno™**

Sept. 12, 1996 - **Sly™**
Sept. 16, 1995 - **Derby™**
Sept. 16, 1995 - **Kiwi™**
Sept. 18, 1995 - **Tusk™**
Sept. 21, 1997 - **Stretch™**
Sept. 27, 1998 - **Roam™**
Sept. 29, 1997 - **Stinger™**

October

Oct. 1, 1997 - **Smoochy™**
Oct. 2, 1998 - **Butch™**
Oct. 3, 1996 - **Bernie™**
Oct. 3, 1990 - **Germania™**
Oct. 9, 1996 - **Doby™**
Oct. 10, 1997 - **Jabber™**
Oct. 12, 1996 - **Tuffy™**
Oct. 14, 1997 - **Rainbow™**
Oct. 16, 1995 - **Bumble™**

Oct. 17, 1996 - **Dotty™**
Oct. 22, 1996 - **Snip™**
Oct. 28, 1996 - **Spinner™**
Oct. 29, 1996 - **Batty™**
Oct. 30, 1995 - **Radar™**
Oct. 31, 1995 - **Spooky™**
Oct. 31, 1999 - **Sheets™**
Oct. 31, 1998 - **Pumkin'™**

November

Nov. 3, 1997 - **Puffer™**
Nov. 4, 1998 - **Goatee™**
Nov. 6, 1996 - **Pouch™**
Nov. 7, 1997 - **Ants™**

Nov. 9, 1996 - **Congo™**
Nov. 14, 1993 - **Cubbie™**
Nov. 14, 1994 - **Goldie™**
Nov. 18, 1998 - **Goochy™**
Nov. 20, 1997 - **Prance™**
Nov. 21, 1996 - **Nanook™**
Nov. 27, 1996 - **Gobbles™**
Nov. 28, 1995 -
    Teddy™ (brown)
Nov. 29, 1994 - **Inky™**

December

Dec. 2, 1996 - **Jolly™**
Dec. 6, 1997 - **Fortune™**
Dec. 6, 1998 - **Santa™**
Dec. 8, 1996 - **Waves™**
Dec. 12, 1996 - **Blizzard™**
Dec. 14, 1996 - **Seamore™**
Dec. 15, 1997 - **Britannia™**
Dec. 16, 1995 - **Velvet™**
Dec. 19, 1995 - **Waddle™**

Dec. 21, 1996 - **Echo™**
Dec. 22, 1996 - **Snowball™**
Dec. 24, 1995 - **Ziggy™**
Dec. 25, 1996 -
    1997 Teddy™
Dec. 25, 1998 -
    1998 Holiday Teddy™
Dec. 25, 1999 -
    1999 Holiday Teddy™

Beanie Babies® Yearbook

When did your *Beanie Babies* join the collection? You can find out in this *Beanie Babies® Yearbook*. Not only does this section list the *Beanies* in order of the year they were issued, but it also tells you the actual date your *Beanie Babies* joined their friends in the world of Ty.

January 1994

1/8/94.... Brownie™/Cubbie™
    the bear
1/8/94.... Chocolate™ the moose
1/8/94.... Flash™ the dolphin
1/8/94.... Legs™ the frog
1/8/94.... Patti™ the platypus
1/8/94.... Pinchers™ the lobster
1/8/94.... Splash™ the whale
1/8/94.... Spot™ the dog
1/8/94.... Squealer™ the pig

June 1994

6/25/94... Ally™ the alligator
6/25/94... Blackie™ the bear

6/25/94... Bones™ the dog
6/25/94... Chilly™ the polar bear
6/25/94... Daisy™ the cow
6/25/94... Digger™ the crab
6/25/94... Goldie™ the goldfish
6/25/94... Happy™ the hippo
6/25/94... Humphrey™ the camel
6/25/94... Inky™ the octopus
6/25/94... Lucky™ the ladybug
6/25/94... Mystic™ the unicorn
6/25/94... Peking™ the panda
6/25/94... Quackers™ the duck

June 1994, cont.

6/25/94... Seamore™ the seal
6/25/94... Slither™ the snake
6/25/94... Speedy™ the turtle
6/25/94... Teddy™ (brown)
    the bear
6/25/94... Teddy™ (cranberry)
    the bear
6/25/94... Teddy™ (jade) the bear
6/25/94... Teddy™ (magenta)
    the bear
6/25/94... Teddy™ (teal) the bear
6/25/94... Teddy™ (violet)
    the bear
6/25/94... Trap™ the mouse
6/25/94... Web™ the spider

January 1995

1/7/95.... Nip™ the cat
1/7/95.... Valentino™ the bear
1/7/95.... Zip™ the cat

June 1995

6/3/95.... Bessie™ the cow
6/3/95.... Bronty™
    the brontosaurus
6/3/95.... Bubbles™ the fish
6/3/95.... Bumble™ the bee
6/3/95.... Caw™ the crow
6/3/95.... Coral™ the fish
6/3/95.... Derby™ the horse
6/3/95.... Flutter™ the butterfly
6/3/95.... Inch™ the inchworm

JUNE 1995, CONT.

6/3/95. . . . Kiwi™ the toucan
6/3/95. . . . Lizzy™ the lizard
6/3/95. . . . Magic™ the dragon
6/3/95. . . . Nana™/Bongo™
    the monkey
6/3/95. . . . Peanut™ the elephant
6/3/95. . . . Pinky™ the flamingo
6/3/95. . . . Rex™ the tyrannosaurus
6/3/95. . . . Steg™ the stegosaurus
6/3/95. . . . Sting™ the stingray
6/3/95. . . . Stinky™ the skunk
est. 6/3/95 . Stripes™ the tiger
6/3/95. . . . Tabasco™ the bull
est. 6/3/95 . Tusk™ the walrus
6/3/95. . . . Velvet™ the panther
6/3/95. . . . Waddle™ the penguin
6/3/95. . . . Ziggy™ the zebra

SEPTEMBER 1995

9/1/95. . . . Radar™ the bat
9/1/95. . . . Spooky™ the ghost

JANUARY 1996

1/7/96. . . . Bucky™ the beaver
1/7/96. . . . Chops™ the lamb
1/7/96. . . . Ears™ the rabbit
1/7/96. . . . Flip™ the cat
1/7/96. . . . Garcia™ the bear
1/7/96. . . . Grunt™ the razorback
1/7/96. . . . Hoot™ the owl
1/7/96. . . . Manny™ the manatee
1/7/96. . . . Ringo™ the raccoon
1/7/96. . . . Seaweed™ the otter
est. 1/7/96 . Tank™ the armadillo
1/7/96. . . . Twigs™ the giraffe
1/7/96. . . . Weenie™
    the dachshund

JUNE 1996

6/15/96. . . Congo™ the gorilla
6/15/96. . . Curly™ the bear

JUNE 1996, CONT.

6/15/96. . . Freckles™ the leopard

6/15/96. . . Lefty™ the donkey
6/15/96. . . Libearty™ the bear
6/15/96. . . Righty™ the elephant
6/15/96. . . Rover™ the dog
6/15/96. . . Scoop™ the pelican
6/15/96. . . Scottie™
    the Scottish terrier
6/15/96. . . Sly™ the fox
6/15/96. . . Sparky™ the dalmatian
6/15/96. . . Spike™ the rhinoceros
6/15/96. . . Wrinkles™ the bulldog

JANUARY 1997

1/1/97. . . . Bernie™ the St. Bernard
1/1/97. . . . Crunch™ the shark
1/1/97. . . . Doby™ the Doberman
1/1/97. . . . Fleece™ the lamb
1/1/97. . . . Floppity™ the bunny
1/1/97. . . . Gracie™ the swan
1/1/97. . . . Hippity™ the bunny
1/1/97. . . . Hoppity™ the bunny
1/1/97. . . . Maple™ the bear
1/1/97. . . . Mel™ the koala
1/1/97. . . . Nuts™ the squirrel
1/1/97. . . . Pouch™ the kangaroo
1/1/97. . . . Snip™ the Siamese cat
1/1/97. . . . Snort™ the bull

MAY 1997

5/11/97. . . Baldy™ the eagle
5/11/97. . . Blizzard™ the tiger
5/11/97. . . Chip™ the cat
5/11/97. . . Claude™ the crab

MAY 1997, CONT.

5/11/97... Doodle™ the rooster
5/11/97... Dotty™ the dalmatian
5/11/97... Echo™ the dolphin
5/11/97... Jolly™ the walrus
5/11/97... Nanook™ the husky
5/11/97... Peace™ the bear
5/11/97... Pugsly™ the pug dog
5/11/97... Roary™ the lion
5/11/97... Tuffy™ the terrier
5/11/97... Waves™ the whale

JULY 1997

7/12/97... Strut™ the rooster

OCTOBER 1997

10/1/97... 1997 Teddy™ the bear
10/1/97... Batty™ the bat

10/1/97... Gobbles™ the turkey
10/1/97... Snowball™
             the snowman
10/1/97... Spinner™ the spider
10/29/97.. Princess™ the bear

DECEMBER 1997

12/31/97.. Britannia™ the bear
12/31/97.. Bruno™ the dog
12/31/97.. Hissy™ the snake
12/31/97.. Iggy™ the iguana
12/31/97.. Pounce™ the cat
12/31/97.. Prance™ the cat
12/31/97.. Puffer™ the puffin
12/31/97.. Rainbow™
             the chameleon
12/31/97.. Smoochy™ the frog

DECEMBER 1997, CONT.

12/31/97.. Spunky™
             the cocker spaniel
12/31/97.. Stretch™ the ostrich

JANUARY 1998

1/31/98... Erin™ the bear

MAY 1998

5/1/98.... Clubby™ the bear
5/30/98... Ants™ the anteater
5/30/98... Early™ the robin
5/30/98... Fetch™
             the golden retriever
5/30/98... Fortune™ the panda
5/30/98... GiGi™ the poodle
5/30/98... Glory™ the bear
5/30/98... Jabber™ the parrot
5/30/98... Jake™ the mallard duck
5/30/98... KuKu™ the cockatoo
5/30/98... Rocket™ the blue jay
5/30/98... Stinger™ the scorpion
5/30/98... Tracker™
             the basset hound
5/30/98... Whisper™ the deer
5/30/98... Wise™ the owl

SEPTEMBER 1998

9/26/98... Billionaire Bear™
             the bear
9/30/98... 1998 Holiday Teddy™
             the bear
9/30/98... Beak™ the kiwi
9/30/98... Canyon™ the cougar
9/30/98... Halo™ the angel bear
9/30/98... Loosy™ the goose
9/30/98... Pumkin'™ the pumpkin
9/30/98... Roam™ the buffalo
9/30/98... Santa™ the elf
9/30/98... Scorch™ the dragon
9/30/98... Zero™ the penguin

DECEMBER 1998

12/12/98. . #1 Bear™ the bear

JANUARY 1999

1/1/99. . . . 1999 Signature Bear™
    the bear
1/1/99. . . . Butch™ the bull terrier
1/1/99. . . . Eggbert™ the chick
1/1/99. . . . Ewey™ the lamb
1/1/99. . . . Fuzz™ the bear
1/1/99. . . . Germania™ the bear
1/1/99. . . . Goatee™
    the mountain goat
1/1/99. . . . Goochy™ the jellyfish
1/1/99. . . . Hippie™ the bunny
1/1/99. . . . Hope™ the bear
1/1/99. . . . Kicks™ the bear
1/1/99. . . . Luke™ the black lab
1/1/99. . . . Mac™ the cardinal
1/1/99. . . . Millennium™ the bear
1/1/99. . . . Mooch™
    the spider monkey
1/1/99. . . . Nibbler™ the rabbit
1/1/99. . . . Nibbly™ the rabbit
1/1/99. . . . Prickles™ the hedgehog
1/1/99. . . . Sammy™ the bear
1/1/99. . . . Scat™ the cat
1/1/99. . . . Slippery™ the seal
1/1/99. . . . Stilts™ the stork
1/1/99. . . . Tiny™ the Chihuahua
1/1/99. . . . Valentina™ the bear

MARCH 1999

3/31/99. . . Clubby II™ the bear

APRIL 1999

4/8/99. . . . Eucalyptus™ the koala
4/8/99. . . . Neon™ the seahorse
4/8/99. . . . Pecan™ the bear
4/11/99. . . Schweetheart™
    the orangutan

APRIL 1999, CONT.

4/12/99. . . Paul™ the walrus
4/14/99. . . Knuckles™ the pig
4/14/99. . . Swirly™ the snail
4/16/99. . . Tiptoe™ the mouse
4/17/99. . . Cheeks™ the baboon
4/17/99. . . Osito™ the bear
4/19/99. . . Almond™ the bear
4/20/99. . . Amber™ the cat
4/21/99. . . Silver™ the cat
4/22/99. . . Wiser™ the owl
4/24/99. . . Spangle™ the bear

SUMMER 1999

Summer . . B.B. Bear™ the bear

Summer . . Flitter™ the butterfly
Summer . . Lips™ the fish

AUGUST 1999

8/31/99. . . 1999 Holiday Teddy™
    the bear
8/31/99. . . Chipper™ the chipmunk
8/31/99. . . Groovy™ the bear
8/31/99. . . Honks™ the goose
8/31/99. . . Scaly™ the lizard
8/31/99. . . Sheets™ the ghost
8/31/99. . . Slowpoke™ the sloth
8/31/99. . . The End™ the bear
8/31/99. . . Ty 2K™ the bear
8/31/99. . . Wallace™ the bear

SEPTEMBER 1999

9/12/99. . . Billionaire™ #2
    the bear

INDEX BY
ANIMAL TYPE

This section offers an easy way to locate your *Beanie Babies*, *Buddies* and *Teenies* in our Value Guide. Once you find the animal you're looking for, just turn to the page!

INDEX BY ANIMAL TYPE

INDEX BY ANIMAL TYPE

(BD) = Beanie
Buddies®

(TB) = Teenie
Beanie Babies™

COLLECTOR'S CHECKLIST BY TAG GENERATION

CURRENT BEANIE BABIES®

	1	2	3	4	5
❑ 1999 Holiday Teddy™					●
❑ 1999 Signature Bear™					●
❑ Almond™					●
❑ Amber™					●
❑ B.B. Bear™					●
❑ Beak™					●
❑ Butch™					●
❑ Cheeks™					●
❑ Chipper™					●
❑ Clubby II™					●
❑ Early™					●
❑ Eucalyptus™					●
❑ Flitter™					●
❑ Fuzz™					●
❑ Germania™					●
❑ GiGi™					●
❑ Goatee™					●
❑ Goochy™					●
❑ Groovy™					●
❑ Halo™					●
❑ Honks™					●
❑ Hope™					●
❑ Jabber™					●
❑ Jake™					●
❑ Kicks™					●
❑ Knuckles™					●
❑ KuKu™					●
❑ Lips™					●
❑ Luke™					●
❑ Mac™					●
❑ Maple™ ("Maple™" tush tag)				●	●
❑ Millennium™ ("Millennium™" on both tags)					●
❑ Mooch™					●

CURRENT BEANIE BABIES®, CONT.

	1	2	3	4	5
❑ Neon™					●
❑ Osito™					●
❑ Paul™					●
❑ Pecan™					●
❑ Prickles™					●
❑ Roam™					●
❑ Rocket™					●
❑ Sammy™					●
❑ Scaly™					●
❑ Scat™					●
❑ Schweetheart™					●
❑ Scorch™					●
❑ Sheets™					●
❑ Silver™					●
❑ Slippery™					●
❑ Slowpoke™					●
❑ Spangle™ (blue face)					●
❑ Spangle™ (red face)					●
❑ Spangle™ (white face)					●
❑ Swirly™					●
❑ The End™					●
❑ Tiny™					●
❑ Tiptoe™					●
❑ Tracker™					●
❑ Ty 2K™					●
❑ Valentina™					●
❑ Wallace™					●
❑ Whisper™					●

RETIRED BEANIE BABIES®

	1	2	3	4	5
❑ #1 Bear™	Special Tag			●	
❑ 1997 Teddy™					●
❑ 1998 Holiday Teddy™					●
❑ Ally™	●	●	●	●	
❑ Ants™					●

RETIRED BEANIE BABIES®, CONT.

	1	2	3	4	5
Baldy				●	●
Batty (tie-dye)					●
Batty (brown)				●	●
Bernie				●	●
Bessie			●	●	
Billionaire Bear	**Special Tag**				
Billionaire #2	**Special Tag**				
Blackie	●	●	●	●	●
Blizzard				●	●
Bones	●	●	●	●	●
Bongo (tan tail)				●	●
Bongo (brown tail)			●	●	
Britannia					●
Bronty			●		
Brownie	●				
Bruno					●
Bubbles			●	●	
Bucky			●	●	
Bumble			●	●	
Canyon					●
Caw			●		
Chilly	●	●	●		
Chip				●	●
Chocolate	●	●	●	●	●
Chops			●	●	
Claude				●	●
Clubby					●
Congo				●	●
Coral			●	●	
Crunch				●	●
Cubbie	●	●	●	●	
Curly				●	●
Daisy	●	●	●	●	●
Derby (star/fluffy mane)					●
Derby (star/coarse mane)					●
Derby (no star/coarse mane)			●	●	

RETIRED BEANIE BABIES®, CONT.

	1	2	3	4	5
Derby (no star/fine mane)			●		
Digger (red)				●	●
Digger (orange)	●	●	●		
Doby				●	●
Doodle				●	
Dotty				●	●
Ears			●	●	●
Echo				●	●
Eggbert					●
Erin					●
Ewey					●
Fetch					●
Flash	●	●	●	●	
Fleece				●	●
Flip				●	●
Floppity				●	●
Flutter			●		
Fortune					●
Freckles				●	●
Garcia				●	●
Glory					●
Gobbles				●	●
Goldie	●	●	●	●	●
Gracie				●	●
Grunt			●		
Happy (lavender)				●	●
Happy (gray)	●	●	●		
Hippie					●
Hippity				●	●
Hissy					●
Hoot			●	●	
Hoppity				●	●
Humphrey	●	●	●		
Iggy (blue/no tongue)					●
Iggy (tie-dye/with tongue)					●
Iggy (tie-dye/no tongue)					●
Inch (yarn antennas)				●	●

RETIRED BEANIE BABIES®, CONT.

	1	2	3	4	5
Inch™ (felt antennas)			●	●	
Inky™ (pink)			●	●	●
Inky™ (tan/with mouth)		●	●		
Inky™ (tan/without mouth)	●	●			
Jolly™				●	●
Kiwi™			●	●	
Lefty™				●	
Legs™		●	●	●	
Libearty™				●	
Lizzy™ (blue)			●	●	●
Lizzy™ (tie-dye)			●		
Loosy™					●
Lucky™ (11 spots)				●	●
Lucky™ (21 spots)				●	
Lucky™ (7 spots)	●	●	●		
Magic™ (pale pink thread)			●	●	
Magic™ (hot pink thread)				●	
Manny™			●	●	
Maple™ ("Pride™" tush tag)				●	
Mel™				●	●
Millennium™ ("Millenium™" swing tag & "Millennium™" tush tag)					●
Millennium™ ("Millenium™" on both tags)					●
Mystic™ (iridescent horn/fluffy mane)					●
Mystic™ (iridescent horn/coarse mane)				●	●
Mystic™ (brown horn/coarse mane)			●	●	
Mystic™ (brown horn/fine mane)	●	●	●		
Nana™			●		
Nanook™				●	●

RETIRED BEANIE BABIES®, CONT.

	1	2	3	4	5
Nibbler™					●
Nibbly™					●
Nip™ (white paws)			●	●	●
Nip™ (all gold)			●		
Nip™ (white face)		●	●		
Nuts™				●	●
Patti™ (magenta)			●	●	●
Patti™ (maroon)	●	●	●		
Peace™				●	●
Peanut™ (light blue)			●	●	●
Peanut™ (dark blue)			●		
Peking™	●	●	●		
Pinchers™ ("Pinchers™" swing tag)	●	●	●	●	●
Pinchers™ ("Punchers™" swing tag)	●				
Pinky™			●	●	●
Pouch™				●	●
Pounce™					●
Prance™					●
Princess™ (P.E. pellets)				●	
Princess™ (P.V.C. pellets)				●	
Puffer™					●
Pugsly™				●	●
Pumkin'™					●
Quackers™ ("Quackers™"/with wings)		●	●	●	●
Quackers™ ("Quacker™"/without wings)	●	●			
Radar™			●	●	
Rainbow™ (tie-dye/with tongue)					●
Rainbow™ (blue/no tongue)					●
Rex™			●		
Righty™				●	
Ringo™			●	●	●
Roary™				●	●

RETIRED BEANIE BABIES®, CONT.

Name	1	2	3	4	5
Rover				●	●
Santa					●
Scoop				●	●
Scottie				●	●
Seamore		●	●	●	●
Seaweed			●	●	●
Slither	●	●	●		
Sly (white belly)				●	●
Sly (brown belly)				●	
Smoochy					●
Snip				●	●
Snort				●	●
Snowball				●	
Sparky				●	
Speedy	●	●	●	●	
Spike				●	●
Spinner ("Spinner" tush tag)				●	●
Spinner ("Creepy" tush tag)					●
Splash	●	●	●	●	
Spooky ("Spooky" swing tag)				●	●
Spooky ("Spook" swing tag)				●	
Spot (with spot)			●	●	●
Spot (without spot)	●	●			
Spunky					●
Squealer	●	●	●	●	●
Steg				●	
Stilts					●
Sting				●	●
Stinger					●
Stinky			●	●	●
Stretch					●
Stripes (light w/ fewer stripes)				●	●
Stripes (dark w/ fuzzy belly)				●	

RETIRED BEANIE BABIES®, CONT.

Name	1	2	3	4	5
Stripes (dark w/ more stripes)			●		
Strut				●	●
Tabasco				●	●
Tank (9 plates/ with shell)				●	
Tank (9 plates/ without shell)				●	
Tank (7 plates/ without shell)			●		
Teddy (brown/new face)		●	●	●	
Teddy (brown/old face)	●	●			
Teddy (cranberry/new face)			●	●	
Teddy (cranberry/old face)	●	●			
Teddy (jade/new face)			●	●	
Teddy (jade/old face)	●	●			
Teddy (magenta/new face)			●	●	
Teddy (magenta/old face)	●	●			
Teddy (teal/new face)			●	●	
Teddy (teal/old face)	●	●			
Teddy (violet/new face)			●	●	
Teddy (violet/new face/ employee bear with red tush tag)	No Swing Tag				
Teddy (violet/old face)	●	●			
Trap	●	●	●		
Tuffy				●	●
Tusk ("Tusk" swing tag)				●	●
Tusk ("Tuck" swing tag)					●

RETIRED BEANIE BABIES®, CONT.

	1	2	3	4	5
❑ Twigs™			●	●	●
❑ Valentino™		●	●	●	●
❑ Velvet™			●	●	
❑ Waddle™			●	●	●
❑ Waves™				●	●
❑ Web™		●	●	●	
❑ Weenie™			●	●	●
❑ Wise™					●

RETIRED BEANIE BABIES®, CONT.

	1	2	3	4	5
❑ Wiser™					●
❑ Wrinkles™				●	●
❑ Zero™					●
❑ Ziggy™			●	●	●
❑ Zip™ (white paws)			●	●	●
❑ Zip™ (all black)			●		
❑ Zip™ (white face)	●	●			

CURRENT BEANIE BUDDIES™

❑ Amber™	❑ Halo™	❑ Peanut™	❑ Snort™
❑ Bongo™	❑ Hippity™	❑ Peking™	❑ Snowboy™
❑ Britannia™	❑ Hope™	❑ Pinky™	❑ Spangle™
❑ Bubbles™	❑ Humphrey™	❑ Princess™	❑ Spinner™
❑ Chilly™	❑ Inch™	❑ Pumkin'™	❑ Squealer™
❑ Chip™	❑ Jabber™	❑ Rover™	❑ Stretch™
❑ Erin™	❑ Jake™	❑ Schweetheart™	❑ Teddy™
❑ Fetch™	❑ Maple™	❑ Silver™	❑ Tracker™
❑ Fuzz™	❑ Millennium™	❑ Slither™	❑ Waddle™
❑ Gobbles™	❑ Peace™	❑ Smoochy™	

RETIRED BEANIE BUDDIES™

❑ Beak™	❑ Quackers™	❑ Quackers™	❑ Twigs™
❑ Patti™	(with wings)	(without wings)	

RETIRED TEENIE BEANIE BABIES™

❑ 1997 Teenie Beanie Babies™ Complete Set	❑ Bongo™	❑ Goldie™	❑ Quacks™
	❑ Britannia™	❑ Happy™	❑ Rocket™
❑ 1998 Teenie Beanie Babies™ Complete Set	❑ Chip™	❑ Iggy™	❑ Scoop™
	❑ Chocolate™	❑ Inch™	❑ Seamore™
❑ 1999 Teenie Beanie Babies™ Complete Set	❑ Chops™	❑ Lizz™	❑ Smoochy™
	❑ Claude™	❑ Maple™	❑ Snort™
❑ 1999 Teenie Beanie Babies™ International Bears	❑ Doby™	❑ Mel™	❑ Speedy™
	❑ Erin™	❑ 'Nook™	❑ Spunky™
	❑ Freckles™	❑ Nuts™	❑ Stretchy™
❑ Antsy™	❑ Glory™	❑ Patti™	❑ Strut™
❑ Bones™	❑ Glory™ (McDonald's employee bear)	❑ Peanut™	❑ Twigs™
		❑ Pinchers™	❑ Waddle™
		❑ Pinky™	❑ Zip™

ALPHABETICAL INDEX

Below is an alphabetical listing of the *Beanie Babies*, *Beanie Buddies* and *Teenie Beanie Babies*, and the pages on which you can find them in the Value Guide!

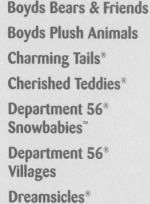